GO BE JESUS

GO BE JESUS

✦

Making Your Mark Through Serving Others

Tony Wolf

iUniverse, Inc.
New York Lincoln Shanghai

GO BE JESUS
Making Your Mark Through Serving Others

iUniverse books may be ordered through booksellers or by contacting:

iUniverse
2021 Pine Lake Road, Suite 100
Lincoln, NE 68512
www.iuniverse.com
1-800-Authors (1-800-288-4677)

Because of the dynamic nature of the Internet, any Web addresses or links contained in this book may have changed since publication and may no longer be valid.

The views expressed in this work are solely those of the author and do not necessarily reflect the views of the publisher, and the publisher hereby disclaims any responsibility for them.
For additional information please visit:
www.tonywolf.com
www.myspace.com/thattonywolfguy

ISBN: 978-0-595-47341-0 (pbk)
ISBN: 978-0-595-91620-7 (ebk)

Printed in the United States of America

For Brooklyn, Katie and Adrienne: the greatest joy you will ever know is helping others.

Contents

Introduction

Jesus Christ never had his name on an office door. He had no placard, no business cards and no typed resume. He didn't have an extension number or e-mail address. He never had Internet access. He didn't have a computer. He didn't even have a cell phone. Jesus had no diplomas or degrees. He never stepped foot onto a Bible college campus. He was never flown in to speak at a convention center, stadium or an arena. He didn't have a concordance or study guides. Jesus never attended a training seminar. He never had access to power point, conferences, sound systems, leadership training, classes or even electricity for that matter. Jesus wasn't in a band, didn't play guitar and never had a record deal. He never signed autographs. He never wrote articles or sold books. Yet, Jesus turned the world upside down through his relationships with eleven men.

We live in a wonderful time. Anything we want or need is almost instantly accessible. Nearly any goal we endeavor to accomplish is relatively easy when we are committed to attaining it. Computer technology allows us to learn anything we need to know. Websites teach us how to prepare barbecue marlin with spicy yellow rice and avocado puree in a matter of minutes. The Internet makes it possible to earn a Masters degree in criminal justice without leaving your home. Self-improvement books are everywhere. Spiritual journals, devotionals and books on Christian living fill the shelves at bookstores. Want to learn about real estate? Seminars, audio books and videos are just a few places to start. We can become experts in creating intricate scrapbooks, speaking foreign languages or replacing car stereos with minimal effort. We have planes, trains and automobiles to take us anywhere in a few minutes or hours most of the time. We have planners and day-timers, we carry Palms and BlackBerry's and we have secretaries to remind us of the critical "who's, what's, where's and when's."

Jesus had none of these advantages. If anything, he dealt with countless obstacles we never have to think about. Still, 2,000 years after his crucifixion he remains the most influential person who ever lived. While one could argue that he had the advantage of being God, he was also completely human. He was a man of flesh and blood. He had to eat, sleep and he certainly got sick sometimes. He undoubtedly experienced muscle cramps, sore feet, splinters, headaches and ingrown nails. He laughed, coughed, sneezed, cried and caught colds. His patience wore thin at times and he certainly must have felt unappreciated at times. He was, and is still, misunderstood by many. At times, he probably didn't feel like doing ministry. His elders were more demanding, critical and demeaning than any of us could imagine. He not only dealt with the temptations that we do, he also came face to face with Satan. Jesus had every opportunity to complain, cite being "burned out" and quit or simply resign from his ministry. Instead, in selflessness, he changed the world by leading eleven men and touching every person he met. In doing so, Jesus continues to change generation after generation since his crucifixion and resurrection. Jesus was God and Jesus was man. Jesus made a difference as a servant.

I have great respect for those who are hired church staff members. It requires a certain type of mental toughness, a level of diplomacy and a skin density that I found extremely difficult. It is challenging, often heartbreaking, thankless, and it is certainly an exposed existence. Beyond the decisions you make, your expressions, appearance and every word are open targets for the criticism of those who you lead. It is a brutal arena. After eight years of located ministry, I realized that I wasn't supposed to have an office door anymore. In the midst of my worship and youth ministry in Tampa, I lacked many traits vital to excelling within its confines. While I may again someday, I no longer have a church office, but I am still using my gifts to serve God. Many of you may be in a similar same place. For example, if you work with students, you give many hours of your week preparing lessons, attending youth events, driving teens to concerts and anything else you can do to help minister to the needs of the youth at your church. You make posters, order pizzas, play football and go along to concerts that make your brains begin to seep out of your ears. You anonymously pay so that teens can to go to conventions. You sacrifice family time with your own children to invest in the lives of young people you are just getting to know. You stay up at night praying for them and with them as well. You aren't paid. You don't receive praise or thanks. You probably never think about it. However, office door or not, you are an invaluable part of God's work. Vocational or not, we all have a job to do as Christians. Fortunately for us, we are not expected to be as influential as the Son of God. Even Paul, who converted many and wrote half of the New Testament, didn't consider equality with God as attainable. However, we should serve others with what we have. It is in this service that people can catch glimpses of Jesus in us.

The gifts we have are his and we have them because he gave them to us. Since they are his, he can do phenomenal things with them. He gives us these gifts so that they might multiply and touch others. Once while leading worship at a camp in eastern Tennessee, I met a young girl, probably in 6th grade or so, who was playing a guitar. She sat on the floor with some tablatures (chord diagrams), teaching herself choruses. As I listened, I was surprised by how well she played and even more impressed with her singing. I asked her, "Would you like to help me lead worship tomorrow night?" You would have thought that I had offered her $1,000.00. She lit up, "Me? You want me to help you?" I said, "Why not?" Beside herself in excitement, she hurried away to practice. I walked away thinking, "Why did I do that? What was I thinking? What if she freezes? What if she's out of tune or plays the wrong chords? What if it disrupts worship?" God had other ideas. As we facilitated worship that night, she was flawless. Ironically, by the end of the night I felt privileged to have played along side her. It was a great night that God would continue to work through and use. Years later I was back at that same camp leading worship again. After services, a tall, confident college girl approached me. "Tony," she said, "Years ago you asked me lead worship with you. I can't tell you what that meant to me." She went on to tell me that she was a music-major and planned to make music her life. She gave me a demo on which she sang, played numerous instruments and produced songs that she had written. It sounded like the property of a seasoned professional. Recently I learned that she now performs often and top Christian recording companies are pursuing her. It is clear to me that I did nothing more than host God's work. I didn't know why I asked her, but God sure did. God will use Leslie to reach a ton of people that I will never meet.

Reading this book you may say, "I can't play a guitar, I'm not a very good speaker, I'm not creative, I don't have abilities." First, many, if not most, people in the Bible considered themselves incapable of doing anything important for God. In their defense, they were incapable. Their God, however, was more than capable. If you can walk, talk or breathe, you have ability. The Bible says in 1 Corinthians 7:7, *"Each one has his own gift from God, one in this manner and another in that."* We serve a God who slays giants with teenaged boys. We serve a God whose Son conquered three days of death. What can he do with you? The answer is simple; whatever he wants and whatever you allow. Moses was a man. The Apostle Paul, Martin Luther King, Billy Graham; each of these men submitted their lives to God's will. Each of these men did some incredible things without being gifted songwriters, athletes or actors. They had one thing in common; the God they served. With a sheepish grin, one of my Bible college professors once told me, "If God can speak through Balaam's Ass, then God can speak through you too." That may be a rough way of putting it, but it is true.

Secondly, God doesn't just move through our abilities, but through our availability as well. He can penetrate hearts through the words of our mouths. He gives us thoughts that can revolutionize our ability to evangelize. He can touch millions with a simple phrase; I have experienced it. As an 18 year-old, I accompanied my youth minister and his band to lead worship at a convention in Charlottesville, Virginia. The night before the convention started, we unloaded our gear, went to sound check, had dinner and checked into our hotel. After using the hotel pool and sauna, we were relaxing in our room, watching a basketball game when there was a knock on the door. We opened the door to find a young man with a guitar. He wore no shoes, hadn't shaved in days and seemed a bit awkward. He introduced himself as the concert artist and wanted permission from us, as the worship leaders, to close out his concert with a worship song of his own. He said, "If you guys wouldn't mind, I'd like to close the concert with a song that they can sing. That might be a little corny, but would you guys listen to the song and tell me what you think?" What could we say? We invited him in and he sat down on the corner of one of our beds and sang a new chorus he'd recently written. He told us he might record it if the verses turned out. He would only perform the chorus the next night at the convention. He would gage the crowd's reaction to determine if he would continue to use the song. The man was Rich Mullins. The song was "Awesome God." Rich wasn't sure if he would use the song long term, but God already knew that he would move millions with this simple chorus for years to come. God clearly gave Rich that song.

My prayer is that this book serves as an encouragement to you. In Ephesians 3:20 Paul says, *"God can do anything, you know—far more than you could ever imagine or guess or request in your wildest dreams! He does it not by pushing us around but by working within us, his Spirit deeply and gently within us."* How much can you imagine? Just how wild can you dream? I would encourage you to think bigger. God is constantly moving and he wants you to use the ability he has given you. He wants to impact others through your service. He knows that if he can use you, lives will change. He believed in you enough to send his son to die for your sin. He knows that with his help, you are capable of all things possible and impossible and you don't have to have a Masters degree in Theology to do it. Jesus never had his name on an office door. His impact was as a servant and only as servants will we make an eternal difference. God can do anything. You can help.

1

"SOME PEOPLE HAVE TO LEARN THE HARD WAY"

God has a plan for your life. No matter where you came from, where you are now or how you are using the gift of life he gave you, he has a plan for you. I didn't know it for a long time, but he has a plan for me too. There were, however, many potholes I ran over on my trip towards that realization. Like many people, I subconsciously adopted backwards ideas about the life of a Christian. We are, largely, a self-seeking people. It is a natural tendency to love your neighbor as you love yourself unless that inconveniences you. The first step towards his plan for your life is to understand that it is his plan. If we are going to make a difference in his kingdom, we must realize that we are servants of the king, not the king ourselves. Furthermore, we must embrace the philosophy of Jesus who instructed the Pharisees that greatness is all about loving God and loving our neighbors. The concept is easy to preach yet difficult for us to practice at all times. I struggled with living as a servant for many years and even now, I must decide to serve every time the opportunities present themselves.

I was adopted at birth in western Maryland in 1968. Some people look at adoption like being the last kid picked in kick ball; I never did. For me, it was much more like the story of Moses. Thanks to my adopting parents, a childhood in Pharaoh's palace couldn't have been much better. Make no mistake, growing up on the income of a printer, I never had my own chariot, never had a chest of gold and I never had access to an entire kingdom as Moses' fortunes provided. What I did inherit was a 77 Ford Maverick, a ton of albums and 45's and, growing up in the 70's, I also had what seemed like the world in the palm of my hand—that's right, I had an Atari. Now years of video pong can be blamed every time I draw a blank, forget something important or daydream myself into a drool. Despite my humble beginnings materialistically, I feel blessed to have had all of my needs provided, necessary discipline when needed and unconditional love as well. I look back now appreciating the plan that God had for my life. Regardless of where we are or what we're doing, God has a plan for us all. I truly understand Psalms 139:13–16; *"For You formed my inward parts; You wove me in my mother's womb. I will give thanks to You, for I am fearfully and wonderfully made; Wonderful are Your works, And my soul knows it very well. My frame was not hidden from You, When I was made in secret, and skillfully wrought in the depths of the earth; Your eyes have seen my unformed substance; And in Your book were all written the days that were ordained for me, when as yet there was not one of them."*

My first experience with church was through Vacation Bible School, weeks of camp and activities at a small Non-denominational Christian church on the Mason-Dixon line. My family is hard to describe, yet very common when it comes to church attendance. My best description of my family and I, in all fairness, would be "Chicken Dinner Softball Christians". My father would realize that there was a fried chicken dinner at church and say, "Get in the truck. They're having chicken at church after service and we're going." Mom would love it when some Southern Gospel group was coming in to perform a concert. My friends and I used to love these groups because they all had that one guy that sang amazingly low and ridiculously loud. We would always laugh whenever the bass guy would brake off some crazy phrase six octaves below everyone else; and yes, we were laughing at them, not with them, there's a big difference. Softball season would roll around and I would try to lay a guilt trip on my parents for not going, knowing that you couldn't play on the church team if you weren't there at least twice a month. At age fifteen, I wanted to go every Sunday because I knew that this beautiful, new girl, Marcy, was going to be there each week. Between cantatas, chili cook-offs and the occasional ministerial firing's, hiring's and resignations under mysterious circumstances, we all had our motives for wanting to be there on any given Sunday. However, I never really met Jesus until shortly before I turned sixteen.

I was flipping quarter-pounders at McDonalds one Sunday night when a friend of mine from church (who, a year later joined me in the grill section as a co-worker at Mickey D's) came in to the restaurant to talk to me. Sean was a strange but talented guy. He and I hit it off at an early age because we both did impersonations. As a kid, I was a big fan of Rich Little. After seeing several of his performances, I started enrolling in school talent shows doing my best Porky Pig, Sylvester the Cat, Muhammid Ali and Darth Vader. I brought my show to Sunday school as well. Sean would always chime right in with his imitation of David Lee Roth, Howard Cosell or Woody Woodpecker. Our Sunday school teacher was an older woman named Mrs. Palmer. She was one of the sweetest ladies I've ever met. While she tried to direct the class to the book of Luke, we would be belting out a scene from Popeye meets Barney Rubble. The class would be chaotic at best. The other kids' laughter just egged us on. While we would take up half of her class time, she would always encourage us (on the weeks that we weren't asked to leave class, that is). She must have danced a naked jig when we moved up from her class to the next.

Sean explained to me that there had been a concert at church. "This wasn't Southern Gospel music," Sean explained, "They played Rock' N Roll and did these hilarious skits, man, it was awesome!" He went on to tell me that this group, called "Son's Up," was going to take forty teenagers on a tour performing an original musical. I wasn't big on musicals or my being in them. Sean told me, "They need a rhythm guitar player so I got some contact info for you." I had been teaching myself guitar for about two years at that point. This was before the law required every youth leader to learn to play the guitar. This was back when the church only had a piano and an organ. As a junior high student, I had watched several pieces on John Lennon after his tragic murder. I was impressed with the effect Lennon and the Beatles had on people. I saw the footage from the legendary Shea Stadium performance where fans were screaming, people were passing out and thousands of girls were crying. This was all the motivation I needed to learn to play. Sometimes God makes good things happen despite our misguided motives. I bought a songbook with tablatures to songs by George Harrison, The Doors, Eagles and other 60's and 70's groups. I learned "Stairway" and "Sweet Home Alabama" and quickly began entertaining family and friends with my out of tune guitar, misplayed chords and awkward breaks. A friend, Mike Shafer, and I performed an awful version of "Norwegian Wood" in our high schools' annual pop concert. There were tuning issues, timing issues and 'Somebody should've loved us enough to stop us' issues. Despite all of these issues, we braved the stage together. While our performance was raw and ill advised, it built my confidence and I was on my way from there. Remembering the fun I'd have at summer church camp and the friends I'd made, I looked at this Son's Up Tour as a two-week break from McDonalds, a chance to meet girls and an opportunity to showcase for the world my guitar talents. Realistically, ten small churches would get to witness my raw guitar skills instead.

I called the leader of the group, Jay Banks, who attended tiny Roanoke Bible College (RBC) in Elizabeth City, North Carolina. By tiny I mean two hundred students, no football team and a handful of graduates each year. Tiny. Shortly after my call, I received a letter of acceptance as a member of the group. Jay, who was also from Maryland, had started a singing group trio in the late seventies that grew into a recruiting powerhouse for the college by the mid-eighties. Jay wrote songs and skits and was a natural at connecting with people through his inspirational ballads. He had signed a contract with Chris Christian and A&M Records on the Bug and Bear label. Jay also had another natural talent that would directly alter my life. Jay had a big influence on young people. Jay was the kind of person who could convince an Oompa Loompa that he could play basketball for the University of North Carolina. Earlier in my life, our church hired a minister, Clyde George, who had that same gift. Clyde made people feel good about who they were. He was very positive and loved young people. He also loved fried chicken so my father loved him. After seeing me in a church play when I was seven or eight, Clyde once got down on his knee, looked me in the eye and said, "Boy, there is nothing that you and God couldn't do together." That one sentence has stuck with me for thirty years. Through Clyde's words I learned how powerful our words of encouragement are. Jay and I hit it off from the start and he was able to encourage me, only he was doing it through a high-powered sound system with phantom power. On the tour, I saw many lives changed in the audience as well as on the stage.

For the next two years of my life, I served as Jay's protégé in located youth ministry. Jay had accepted a position at a church in Raleigh, North Carolina while still serving as Executive Director of Son's Up. We wrote the program for the 1987 Tour together, played ridiculous amounts of basketball and led worship at teen conventions all over the country. Along the way, I met popular Christian artists, played basketball with the Harlem Globetrotters and once found a man's entire thumbnail in an Oreo cookie. The Oreo thing has no relevance here (nor would I consider it impressive), but it did happen that summer and it still bothers me. Jay taught me how to put together a musical and helped me with the fundamentals of midi sequencing and keyboard programming. Nevertheless, in spite of all my training and learning, I wasn't sure what to do. At twenty years old, I was working odd jobs (very odd jobs) and had no idea what should happen next. When I asked Jay about it, he told me I should consider going to Bible College. No one in my family tree had ever gone to college. Jay might just as well have said, "You should try out for the Yankees." Me, go to college? I barely made it through high school. However, after enough people told me that "having a degree will mean that people will take you seriously", I decided to go. How funny is that? That anyone would actually take me seriously. Regardless of my apprehensions, a few months later, with $48 to my name, I was a freshman at RBC.

I had never taken an SAT. Upon my high school graduation, I already had full rides to several art institutions across the country and had gained accepted to numerous universities on the strength of my artwork portfolio without an SAT. I decided that I didn't want to make art a career and, at that point, never thought I would go to college. As a result, I never took the SAT or ACT. Fortunately, RBC did not require an SAT from me. Truthfully, based on the assortment of fruit-cakes, psychos and carnies that surrounded me at freshman orientation, the ability to spell SAT may not have been a requirement. If you are ever feeling low, down or unfortunate, just go to a small Bible College during freshman orientation. Wow. My freshman classmates included a Lucky the Leprechaun look-alike, a bearded lady, a guy who ate pizza with his toes, a 72 year-old woman and a bear. Oh sure, he convinced the financial aids people that he was a Viking, but I knew he was a bear all along. Standing in the middle of the freak show I thought, "I can't believe it. I'm paying thousands of dollars to be in the circus." Over the course of time, I found most of the clowns and jugglers to be fantastic people. Five years later, I would look back and realize that RBC had provided several vital things for me. It provided me the time and a place to mature, biblical knowledge and ministerial experience as well as a lifetime of comedic material (most of which I really can't write about). In truth, I learned more valuable lessons outside the classroom than I did in it. That is not a derogatory statement towards RBC, but a testament to some insightful individuals who I met while I was there.

My first year at Roanoke was rough. I really struggled adopting the concept of selflessness. My grades were just good enough to keep me in school, while the old woman made the deans list and the bear did surprisingly well. I was productive in the areas I enjoyed. I played on the basketball team, wrote songs and skits and dated regularly, but my own immaturity made those areas a struggle as well. One day at basketball practice, I was convinced that a certain offensive set would never work. I proceeded to let it be known in rather loud fashion and was ejected. A game is one thing, but who gets ejected from practice? I was more concerned about people knowing that I wrote my own music than conveying the essential information during performances. I also passed on dating some very godly young women because I was infatuated with physical appearances and insecure about myself.

One of my first pieces of advice to you as you read this book is to learn contentment. Paul wrote to his friends in Philippi, in Philippians 4:11–12, *"I have learned to be content whatever the circumstances. I know what it is to be in need, and I know what it is to have plenty. I have learned the secret of being content in any and every situation."* I am not suggesting that you become complacent or tolerant of mediocrity. What I am saying is to seek out the value and opportunity of each day. Understand that, as you read this, you possess priceless gifts. This day, this time, these breaths are yours only because God is giving them to you. I, almost robotically at times, moved through some irreplaceable days with the heart of the tin woodsman. I wasted many precious chances to influence people on a profound level because I looked at those ministries as steppingstones. I would sing at a small church and think 'I should be playing big arenas.' I felt I was more talented and worthy than some people who had already "made it big" were. Robert Brault once said, "Enjoy the little things in life, for one day you will look back and realize that they were the big things." It's easy for me now to see that my life was dominated by discontent.

Timothy may also have struggled with this. Part of discontentment is natural in our youth, but no matter how old we are, it seems we all deal with it in waves. Paul, again, wrote to Timothy in I Timothy 6:6–12 and said *"But godliness actually is a means of great gain when accompanied by contentment. For we have brought nothing into the world, so we cannot take anything out of it either. If we have food and covering, with these we shall be content. But those who want to get rich fall into temptation and a snare and many foolish and harmful desires, which plunge men into ruin and destruction. For the love of money is a root of all sorts of evil, and some by longing for it have wandered away from the faith and pierced themselves with many griefs. But flee from these things, you man of God, and pursue righteousness, godliness, faith, love, perseverance and gentleness. Fight the good fight of faith; take hold of the eternal life to which you were called, and you made the good confession in the presence of many witnesses."* I may have read this before but it never sunk in. Righteousness and godliness were qualities I had only read about, I had to learn the hard way that "making it" was all about losing it. Lives don't change through our degrees or accolades but through the depth of our character and love for people. In time, I would learn that ministry was more about one-on-one than one in front of thousands.

My first serious lesson came from an unlikely character. The groundskeeper at RBC was a man from eastern North Carolina named Phil Alligood. Being a resident of certain areas in eastern North Carolina is sort of like being from the set of Hee Haw. In fact, Mayberry would look more like inner city Detroit to people from this region. "Alligood", as we all called him, was a loud and energetic man (which were essential qualities for anyone who pushed around a lawnmower 21 hours a day). He was also responsible for building maintenance and repairs. He called me aside one day after chapel. When he said, "Sit down here a minute feller", I knew the conversation wasn't going to end with a hug. "You see that window over there?" he said. He was pointing to a window that I had broken the night before. Roanoke had numerous piano practice rooms in the main building. I would go to these rooms and practice almost every night. Some nights, however, the building would end up locked early. Having little regard for any rules I might be fracturing, I tried to bypass the locked doors by climbing in a cafeteria window. I had done this numerous times before, but on this particular night, I put a hole in the screen and bent it. "That window?" I asked as though I hadn't noticed. Knowing, though I'm still not sure how, that I was the culprit, Alligood glared at me and said, "Tony, I'm concerned for you. You have a great deal of potential son, but the little things define who you are. And the little things are eventually going to be your downfall."

I was hurt. I acted as if I was mad because my ego was too big to reveal a chink in my armor. I felt, at first, as if he was suggesting that I was a bad apple. I thought he said what he said because he generally detested me. However, a few hours later, I began to reason. Perhaps Mr. Alligood took a few minutes to talk to me because he cared. Maybe he actually felt I was worth his time. Maybe he pried himself from his tractor because he saw potential. Maybe he knew the power of encouragement (though I didn't feel encouraged at that moment). Over the next few years, though Alligood and I never exchanged Christmas gifts or anything, I came to know him as a man of honesty and integrity who was making his biggest impact without an office door ... or a lawnmower for that matter. In my case, he probably didn't even realize that he'd made an impression. That's how most people who are making a difference operate. The impact they make is a bi-product of who they are, not what they do. In The Message translation, Paul tells Timothy, *"And don't let anyone put you down because you're young. Teach believers with your life: by word, by demeanor, by love, by faith, by integrity."* The example I was setting was not one of integrity; I was dishonest, aloof and undisciplined. After a few more brainless and juvenile blunders similar to the window caper, our school president, President Griffin, actually advised me to start over at another school. It was right about then that I began to realize I had a lot of growing up to do.

Something I'm realizing increasingly as I grow older is that God seems to teach us the most when we have the least. In an effort to clear my mind and decide what to do next, I went home that summer and worked as a forklift operator for a company called Wetterau. Wetterau was a grocery and produce distributor. They would receive bulk orders from grocery stores for their stock and sales. An operator, like myself, was responsible for pulling a store order, picking the pieces from our warehouse bins, loading and packing the pieces onto a skid and delivering them to trucks on a dock via forklifts. Easy enough, right? It would have been except for a few minor details. First, there was 'The Physical.' To make a long story short, never see a doctor who has the words Louisville Slugger etched onto one of his fingers: Not good. Secondly, I worked the graveyard shift six days a week, which was an adjustment. Finally, warehouses are not for you if you aren't in shape. If I worked there today at an out of shape thirty-nine years old, I'd be in intensive care tomorrow, probably in critical condition. The supervisors demanded that you load three hundred 'pieces' an hour. To put that into perspective that's identifying, finding and loading five items a minute. This was very difficult if the order included items like crates of water, salt bags or bags of dog food that were packed together in 80 pound bags. After your skid was full, you would also have to wrap it and drive it to the proper dock. If in the course of a weeklong period, you averaged two hundred and ninety-nine pieces or less, you lost your job. Routine necessities like going to the bathroom or tying your shoes became a calculated risk whenever you would get behind. Despite a certain level of reasonable trepidation, I put in my first day of work in early June. That's when God began to work on me.

The warehouse bins that contained the products we sold were filthy. They were organized in rows and were stacked three bins high. The bottom bins were always the worst. They were dark, dirty and often contained broken glass, rats, foods, and liquids that had fallen from broken bottles or busted bags. Sometimes food would be down in there for weeks. It was enough to gag a maggot. One night while lifting water out of one of these bottom bins, I felt something I hope to never feel again. A torn groin muscle is a most painful thing that takes place in a most delicate area. I went straight down onto the cold, grimy concrete. As I rolled over onto my back, I remember thinking to myself, "How did I get here?" The obvious answer was this unbearable stinging sensation but my mind quickly went somewhere else. It had to. "Do you know why you are laying here, holding your privates with both hands, rolling around on a nasty, freezing warehouse floor at 4:30 in the morning?" I asked myself. The answer was obvious and it really made me mad. I was there for the same reason that Peter was going under the waters as he walked towards Jesus on the Sea; I wasn't focused on Jesus. I had lost sight of what was critical and it happened gradually, largely because of my irresponsibility with the little things. Alligood was right. That broken window at RBC was only a symptom of a dangerous illness. When I was a young boy, my father used to always say, "It's not the things you do that get you in trouble, it's the things that you don't do that get you in trouble." That was true when I was a kid and, unfortunately, still valid as a young man. I was irresponsible with new jackets, lunch money and homework as a kid and equally negligent with my spirituality as an adult.

Many of us struggle because we aren't responsible with the 'little' things. Instead of 'little', I think more accurate words would actually be essential or crucial or vital. Too often, we fail to realize the importance of our routine daily actions. We blow them off when we become lazy or whenever we have a lethargic or rough day. I will admit, when I was in youth ministry I often found myself procrastinating. Every time I would justify my irresponsibility with excuses. I would say, "It's just a lesson, no big deal." "It's just a class, I'll tell some jokes and skate through it." "It's just a worship service, I've done this hundreds of times, and I don't have to put that much time or thought into it." However, in reality what I was really saying was, "It's just for God, no big deal." "It's just for the cause of Christ, I'll tell some jokes and skate through it." "It's just salvation for those who don't know him, I don't have to put that much time or thought into it." I'm glad Jesus didn't have that attitude when it came to my eternity.

As is always the case, God knew what was best for me. I had planned to travel to numerous Christian camps and conventions that summer, but he knew I needed to be elsewhere. I wasn't supposed to be singing and leading hundreds of people under stage lights, I was supposed to be learning his will in a dark and sullied warehouse. I needed to learn that ministry was about one-on-one not one in front of hundreds. As I lay on the floor in burning groin agony, I thought to myself, "I am never going to be in this position again. I will serve where God puts me, when God sends me with what God has given me." I was off for a week or so to heal but the reality of my position was two more months in the warehouse. I wasn't exactly thrilled but, thankfully, God was listening to my thoughts. He was prepared to use me at Wetterau; right then, with what he had given me and I never saw it coming.

The cast of characters I worked with that summer looked more like Arkham Asylum (the hospital for the criminally insane arch-enemies of Batman) than a workplace. Among them was Jim, a forty-five year old Shaggy look-a-like who would ride his lift up and down the aisles as fast as it would go while doing loud Popeye impersonations for all to hear. While picking orders, I would hear Jim several aisles away yelling, "Whoooaaah!" perfectly mimicking the famous one-eyed sailor man. Stubbs was another crazy friend I met that summer. Stubbs specialized in pretending to be mad at guys just to see their reaction and he was great at it. There were many shrill confrontations that always ended with Stubbs on the floor laughing his butt off while his embarrassed victims would stomp off saying, "That ain't funny man!" I also worked with many ex-convicts, mentally unstable individuals and several drug addicts. One guy, also named Tony, could pick an average of five hundred and forty pieces and hour while the rest of our crew averaged around three sixty. The company knew that Tony was pumping himself full of anti-depressants, but having a guy that could pick nearly twice as fast as anyone else proved invaluable to them could. Guess who would mysteriously always get around company random drug tests? One night another employee brought a gun to work and started waving it around, threatening to kill himself over some family problems. It was scary. Then there were John and Rob.

John used profane words more than he used acceptable ones. He was a rare talent capable of using his favorite 'curse' word eight times in one sentence. He'd use it as a noun, a verb, an adjective, and of course, as an interjection. He was a nice guy otherwise, but was not seeking a spiritual lifestyle; or vocabulary for that matter. However, he and I actually got along very well and ended up working as a team on a few different occasions. We became friends naturally. Once night, seven people called in sick and John and I ended up as the only two operators on the floor. The trucks were also running late so we ended up in the break room awaiting the onslaught of orders to come. We started talking about my college ("Bible" college). John had a ton of questions. It was surprising how little he knew about the Bible or about Jesus. In the weeks to come, we had several more conversations, I loaned him a few books and one day before work, John said to me, "So, how can I become a Christian?" I was shocked. We'd only talked a few times and I had even wondered if John was just humoring me. We sat down and started talking and before I knew what was going on, John was in tears, and asking me to baptize him. We talked a couple more times, he got his girlfriend and some family members together, and we went to a local church one morning after work. In front of a few of his friends and family, he confessed his sins, proclaimed Christ as his Savior and I baptized him. God was teaching me more in a warehouse than I had learned, or would learn, in five years of Bible College … and he wasn't finished.

Rob had been my best friend growing up. We traded videogames, listened to our Run DMC tapes and played sandlot football together almost every weekend. Rob had become increasingly curious about what it meant to be a Christian especially after I ended up training for the ministry. Ironically, Rob ended up needing a job a few weeks after I started at Wetterau so I told my supervisor and Rob's application managed to make it's way to the top of the heap. Rob called to tell me how excited he was about getting the job, "I start next Monday," he said. I told him, "It's going to be great to work together man." However, I didn't tell him about "The Physical." Rob and I spent a lot of time together that summer and after numerous discussions and a couple of Bible studies Rob was ready to take the plunge. His was a relatively simple conversion, but his family was the difficult part. His father was a devout Catholic and his mother was an ultra-conservative Lutheran so naturally there was a lot of discussion coming from very different angles. Baptism was a hot topic. I never understood some people's hesitance towards baptism. I've heard it called a 'work', yet, it is the one thing that a Christ-follower can't do himself. Unlike prayer, witnessing, confessing our sins or asking Christ to be our Lord (all things we do as we follow him), baptism is something done to us by someone else. Jesus subjected himself to it. Jesus told us to do the same. My thinking has always been, as Christ-followers, we all should do the same. The last thing he said to his disciples in Matthew 28 was *"Go, therefore, and make disciples of all nations, baptizing them in the name of the Father and of the Son and of the Holy Spirit, teaching them to observe everything I have commanded you. And remember, I am with you always, to the end of the age."* I read this passage that day. They acted as if they had never heard this before. Shortly thereafter, they proudly watched their son confess Christ as his savior and submit to the waters of baptism. It was a special day for me because Rob and I (both only children) were more like brothers than we were friends. Rob was family to me. God had moved in my life like never before and as a result, my best friend and an unlikely co-worker had acknowledged Jesus as their only hope. I had left my spiritual college surroundings feeling broken and got fixed in a warehouse where broken spirits surrounded me. It was an incredible summer, so much so, that my life has never been the same.

I decided that fall to return to RBC despite the advice of President Griffin. I believe he had my best interest in mind when he gave me that advice but I just saw that as taking the easy way out. I wanted to grow where my gardeners could be proud of my growth. You know, there are not many things more frustrating than buying a plant or a goldfish or some other living thing that costs less than five dollars at Wal-Mart only to watch it die in a few days. However, let that fish, plant, or thing live for an extended period and suddenly you bloom with pride and place it on display that all may behold the wonder of your hanging plant, thirty-cent fish or your precious … 'thing.' I wanted my school to feel good about having me there. I felt I had let certain people down and cast a harmful image on them by their association with me. I wanted to do well to vindicate myself as well as the people who believed in me. Of course, these weren't correct motives. One day at lunch I explained my ambitions to one of my mentors at Roanoke, a graduate minister named Tony Krantz. His input really changed my perspective. Tony said, "You could never please everyone all the time even if you were perfect. Just look how it went for Jesus. Just make sure that his benefit is the motivation behind everything you do and you'll be fine." Tony is the best piano player I had ever met and a good songwriter as well and I looked up to him for that. He is also one of the most intelligent people I've ever met. Frustrated that there was only one television in the student center years ago, Tony once wanted to watch a show so badly that he built his own TV with parts he assembled in a salvage yard. He was building his own home the last time I saw him. I mean he was literally building it, with his own two hands, alone. Tony was an incredibly bright man who gave me incalculable advice and encouragement. The benefit of God's people (which is all of humanity, not just "religious" people) should be our goal in anything we attempt. That's ministry.

One of Son's Up's songs simply said "Less of me and more of you." I tried to place those lyrics in the front of my physically enormous head. I had previously been guilty of having a big head for my somewhat arrogant and ignorant attitude. That was beginning to subside through my failures but I still wore a 7 5/8 sized fitted cap (sometimes 8). Two of my kids in my first youth ministry, Katie and Danielle, used to affectionately call me "Fathead." Despite my Cro-Magnon sized skull, I was asked to be part of several musical groups at college; a rap group called "B.I.C." (Brothas In Christ), a music and drama team called "Spirit" and the schools most popular group, an alternative style band called "Noble Theme." Each time I refused and chose to go my own way. I told each group that I wanted to focus in on writing musicals and such. In retrospect, I think I thought I was somehow better than they were. Not better as a person, but creatively. I saw myself doing "bigger and better" things. I was an arrogant prima Donna and didn't even realize it. However, after encounters with people like Mr. Alligood and President Griffin, a summer at the warehouse and some serious personal reevaluation, it was clear that something had to change. With the "less of me" mentality, I tried to take a different approach.

Garrett Lewis was one of three guys (along with Tim Hunt and Jay) who convinced me that Roanoke was where I needed to be. "Pop" was not only the dean of students, but he was also the coach of our basketball team and in charge of special events on campus. "Pop" was the kind of person that nearly everyone loved. He recruited me and stuck by me throughout my worst moments and I felt terrible about how I made him look. Some people had referred to me as "Pop's Boy" which I never minded. If it wasn't for him we wouldn't have had a basketball team, there would've been no one to teach us how to play serious ping pong and I wouldn't have been at college or lasted more than a month after I got there. Pop had one arm withered by polio when he was an infant yet he still played basketball with us at practice and he played better than most of us. One time one of our players challenged Pop to a free throw contest. My teammate made fifteen in a row. Then Pop stepped to the line and sank sixty-seven consecutive free throws (with what amounted to one arm). During my junior year, Pop was frustrated with the officiating one night. We were leading big late in the game and I was sitting beside him on the bench. He sighed heavily, waved his hand and said "Tony, get in there and do something!" I asked him, "Who do you want me to go in for?" He said "Nobody. Just walk out there." I said, "Pop, it'll be 6-on-5." Pop looked at me and grinned, "They haven't noticed anything else tonight, and I'll bet they don't notice you either." I played for a minute and a half and scored four more points before they noticed and called a technical foul on me. I love Pop.

I asked Pop if I could be part of a recruitment effort called "High School Days." He asked what I had in mind and I told him about my summer. I told him that, with the help of one of my best friends, Larry Simons, and advice from Jay, I had written a musical complete with comedic sketches, live band and a message that I felt would make people really think. Pop was skeptical. I told him that I wanted to touch the prospective students that would be at this event but I also wanted to inspire my classmates to do the same. As I looked around our campus, it looked a lot like Wetterau to me. Many people in both places just needed a nudge in the right direction for God to really work on them and through them. I also knew that ministry wasn't about talent, stage presence or anything outward, it was all about availability. Casting all the students that weren't in the campus limelight, I looked for people that always wanted a chance to minister but never got the opportunity in this arena. A forty-member cast of people with the "less of me" mentality, who had never sung, acted or worked a production before, could do far greater things than the old "more of me" Tony Wolf could do on his own. Mother Teresa once said, "Give yourself fully to God. He will use you to accomplish great things on the condition that you believe much more in his love than in your own weakness." At the worst, I felt that a united labor of love by our student body would result in benefit for Christ. When a group makes a statement, it lessens the role of the individual. That's one of the many beautiful things about the concept of the "church." While I was organizing the effort, our students would ultimately facilitate the ministry that was to take place. I hoped it would be like the Son's Up Tours I had been a part of; lives changed in the audience and on the stage. Pop agreed to give it a chance.

Over the course of the next month, we organized casting meetings, practiced with numerous musicians and met with the forty members to worship together, pray and build community. For once, my efforts weren't about me. My efforts really weren't even about the forty members. The efforts had one motivation and one goal; That God's love would be clear and that everyone who would be there would experience it. I asked five random members to go to Nags Head beach a week before the program to pray. We sat out on the beach for hours talking about the program and our hopes for it, praying and worshiping. Each of us took eight of the cast member's names and went off to pray privately for their contribution to this ministry, their future and their personal needs. We later reconvened and celebrated what God was doing. We believed that God would bless the effort. In the final week, there were last minute changes, dress rehearsals and before we knew it, it was Friday night. The program was entitled "Take a Stand." The production was based on 2 Timothy 1:7–8, *"For God has not given us a spirit of timidity, but of power and love and discipline. Therefore, do not be ashamed of the testimony of our Lord ..."* and the idea was to contrast some of the beliefs and practices of our world with the practices and words of Christ. We were conveying this message to 400 prospective students, mostly high school students. The specifics of the performance seemed secondary to me this time. I was twenty-three years old and, for the first time, had completely turned everything over to him and forty of his servants. Again, most of these cast members weren't great singers, spectacular actors or amazingly talented people; they were simply willing. Most of them already had the "less of me" mindset. Moreover, looking back, the time we spent laughing, praying and talking were far more important than the actual production.

Through that evening and numerous experiences to come, I learned that there is a fine line between performance and ministry. So many times, I had approached ministry by trying to "Wow" those that attended. I would think "These people don't know what they're in for. Just wait until they see how good I am. This will be the performance of a lifetime. They are going to be so impressed." I had been a performer greatly anticipating the applause of the crowd without a passion to impact anyone in an eternal manner. Now I understood that people needed to see how good he was, not how good I was. A great song, powerful message or even a good performance will stay with people for a while, but humble ministry, sincere service and acts of love lead people, faithful and not, towards serving others and to an eternal salvation. He desires acts of love from us, not performances. More important than your education, more awesome than any gift or talent, more necessary than years of experience and far more critical than a degree or ordination is our capacity for willingness and selflessness. 1 Peter 5:5–7 says, *"You younger men, likewise, be subject to your elders; and all of you, clothe yourselves with humility toward one another, for God is opposed to the proud, but gives grace to the humble. Therefore, humble yourselves under the mighty hand of God, that He may exalt you at the proper time, casting all your anxiety on Him, because He cares for you."*

He does care for you. God cares enough for you that he sent his Son from the glories of heaven to the filth of earth. His Son took the world by love, not by force. Jesus wasn't a superstar; he was a servant, modeling greatness through service for us. In John 13, Jesus models leadership and love by bathing the feet of his disciples. John 13:5–17 says, *"Then He poured water into the basin, and began to wash the disciples' feet and to wipe them with the towel with which He was girded. So He came to Simon Peter. He said to Him, "Lord, do You wash my feet?" Jesus answered and said to him, "What I do you do not realize now, but you will understand hereafter." Peter said to Him, "Never shall You wash my feet!" Jesus answered him, "If I do not wash you, you have no part with Me." Simon Peter said to Him, "Lord, then wash not only my feet, but also my hands and my head." Jesus said to him, "He who has bathed needs only to wash his feet, but is completely clean; and you are clean, but not all of you." For He knew the one who was betraying Him; for this reason He said, "Not all of you are clean." So when He had washed their feet, and taken His garments and reclined at the table again, He said to them, "Do you know what I have done to you? "You call Me Teacher and Lord; and you are right, for so I am. "If I then, the Lord and the Teacher, washed your feet, you also ought to wash one another's feet. "For I gave you an example that you also should do as I did to you. "Truly, truly, I say to you, a slave is not greater than his master, nor is one who is sent greater than the one who sent him. "If you know these things, you are blessed if you do them."* In the face of betrayal and the knowledge of his impending crucifixion, Christ found it most important to model service. Instead of focusing on the Law, teaching weighty philosophical points or asking for prayer for himself, Jesus was teaching the most important action a human being can carry out; service. Jesus tells his disciples that there is blessing in coming to understand the importance of serving and living that truth out through helping others.

It was an incredible night. God moved numerous people to come forward and many decisions were made in the audience and on the stage. President Griffin, with tears in his eyes, approached me afterwards and said, "I'm glad you ignored my advice (to leave Roanoke). Thank you for what you did tonight. Welcome back." His words meant a lot but I was more grateful to have just been there. I remembered lying on the dirty warehouse floors of Wetterau and was grateful that even at my dirtiest, in my most broken and cynical moments, God still wanted to use me. I realized as a junior in college that ministry is not about a Bachelors degree in Theology or being a famed performer who entertains thousands or having your name on an office door. True ministry is about humility, service, availability, willingness, authenticity, selflessness and always thinking "less of me." This attitude would serve me in ministry, in personal relationships and even in the corporate world. This is, unfortunately, an attitude that is hard to maintain 24/7. It is easy in times of adversity, fatigue or on busy days to forget. It becomes habit to justify our laziness. It really isn't too difficult to manufacture an alibi for our apathy. It is effortless for us to pass responsibilities from ourselves onto anyone and everyone else. During my located ministries, I would find myself saying, "Am I the only person who works here?" "Why doesn't somebody else do it?" "I'm a minister not a slave." Pretty "Christ-like" huh? It's embarrassing when I realize that some day I will be accountable for every one of my careless words. Being a servant is an every day, every hour and every minute decision. It is not usually easy, but it is always right. It is often thankless, but it is always fulfilling. It is not glamorous, but it is always beautiful. Physicist Albert Einstein said, "Strange is our situation here upon earth. Each of us comes for a short visit, not knowing why; yet sometimes seeming to divine a purpose. From the standpoint of daily life, however, there is one thing we do know: that man is here for the sake of other men."

Jesus summed it up best when he said, in Mark 9:35, *"Anyone who wants to be the first must take last place and be the servant of everyone else."* If you are willing to adopt the "less of me" mentality, you are well on your way to the life 'more abundant' that Jesus also mentioned. Most of you have made this a way of life if you are involved in ministry (with or without an office door) and you are likely ready to dig deep and passionately for your role in God's plan. Still I imagine some of you are frustrated, wondering about the specifics of God's plan for you. You might have no idea where your place is. Be encouraged: Your concerns are natural and your feelings are valid. Your future may have some potholes in the middle of it. Just know that God is in control and let him be your guide. You will make a difference if, and when, you serve.

2

"IT'S YOUR SERVE"

Bible College was a great place for me. The five years that I spent on the Outer Banks were invaluable in many ways. In fact, it would have been more valuable if I had applied myself and been focused on all the right things for the duration of my stay. The price of education is (and was even back then) high. I realize that every month when I get my bill from the College Loan Foundation. At times, as I write out that check, I think "Was it worth it?" However, I have come to realize as my adult life teaches me, the cost of ignorance is momentous. I am grateful for my college education, but life experiences continue to be my greatest educator. The sad thing is, I left college uneducated in some extremely crucial and fundamental areas of my life. More poignantly, I wasn't the only one.

Years earlier, I remember something a minister once said to me. In 1986, I was my youth ministers (Jay's) protégé at a small church in North Carolina and frustrated trying to figure out where I belonged. Before Jay had talked to me about going to college, I worked every odd job imaginable. I had been a paperboy in junior high, flipped burgers at McDonalds in high school for three and a half years and, in my two years in Raleigh I delivered pizzas, worked construction, sold shoes and ended up working as a surveyor for the U.S. Geological Survey. In fact, the experiences I endured with the Survey could make a great book. For about a year, my job was to read and record rainfall and water flow in streams and rivers in the deepest woods that North Carolina has to offer. During my time with the Survey, I was attacked by locusts, found myself searching for anacondas (yes, in North Carolina) and took a screw driver to the hand which had to be removed by another surveyor while we were in the field. The job meant killing snakes, cutting paths to our gages through the woods with a machete and even serving as a flagman on certain days while the team worked on bridges. It was a brutal, monotonous toil spent often times in a full body suit or waders in the summer heat.

One day I left the field early and stopped in to the church to see Jay. The office door was locked as usual (a concept I've never understood) so I knocked and the minister greeted me there. He was a highly educated man with more degrees than a right angle. He was a brilliant man and a nice guy but never seemed to look kindly on the 'uneducated.' There I stood with mud all over my pants and boots, covered in sweat and I asked where Jay was. He told me that Jay had left to go help someone in the church. Then, noting it was only early afternoon, he said, "Shouldn't you be working?" Jokingly and in light on the extreme heat on this day, I said, "That's easy for you to say, sitting in there in your office, in the A.C. eating your lunch behind that desk." Sarcastic humor is the most dangerous form of humor there is. His demeanor totally changed. With a scowl, he said to me, "I have a Master's degree son, I've done my time, I've earned the right to sit behind a desk." Then he shut the door (which, of course, then locked). Knowing him as a good man, I chalked it up to him having a bad day. Still, I walked away from that conversation disgusted. As an imperfect and sinful human being, I have only the grace of God and Jesus' blood to thank for my hope and freedom and I don't feel that I have earned anything; In fact, I am in debt. As Christians, the rights we have 'earned' are best summarized in Ephesians 2:4–9. *"But God, being rich in mercy, because of His great love with which He loved us, even when we were dead in our transgressions, made us alive together with Christ (by grace you have been saved), and raised us up with Him, and seated us with Him in the heavenly places in Christ Jesus, so that in the ages to come He might show the surpassing riches of His grace in kindness toward us in Christ Jesus. For by grace you have been saved through faith; and that not of yourselves, it is the gift of God; not as a result of works, so that no one may boast."* The grace that saves us is the free, undeserved goodness of God; and he saves, not because of our achievements, degrees or trophies, but by his grace and through our faith in Jesus. Salvation does not come to us through any works that we ever did, will, or can do. The ministers' comments didn't seem to model gratitude to me. In his words, I found little meekness or humility. His wasn't the voice of one of God's unassuming servants; in fact, it sounded like boasting to me.

The concept of serving was familiar to me but not a lifestyle. That's not on my mentors, Alma Mater or family; that's on me. Being a servant isn't something you learn or do, it's something you are. Being a Christian isn't something you learn or do, it's something you are. You do things like serve, help and love because of who you are. Recently I attended a youth camp in the Pittsburgh area and met a young lady who was confused. The young lady had planned to go to a Christian College and, upon graduation, enter into full-time Christian service. Her church, however, approached her and told her that their children's pastor was leaving and that they were interested in hiring her to fill his position. She told me this story and said, "I don't know what to do. I don't have any training and I feel that I need an education in order to do an adequate job." She told me this just minutes after praying for and hugging about seven or eight of the kids from her church that had just come forward for prayer following a message. "You don't need a degree to do what you just did," I said. "There are no degrees in caring. There are no classes on empathy, comforting the crying or on God-given rapport." Her face lit up as though that had never occurred to her. She hugged me and scampered off to find her group.

In the next few days, I encouraged her that a college education is a great thing and asked her if her church would help her through school. She sounded as though they would and was really excited at the notion that she wouldn't have to wait to get that rolled piece of paper in four years in order to impact the children she already knew and loved. College is a great thing, but our desire to know the Word inside and out is ultimately more powerful than any degree. Our genuine love for others is more important than all the knowledge and credentials that we compile. Our willingness to reach out to those who are in need far exceeds our academic accomplishments. I went to school with many people who had high GPA's that never understood that. They never really "got it." Fortunately, God has used me through my own immaturity and ignorance. I am still learning through my failures and the humbling experiences in my life (and there have been many).

One of my best friends in the world is a youth minister in Florida who I went to school with. Rick wasn't your typical Bible college student. Rick loved Van Halen, had big hair and laughed at just about everything. Rick was always bucking the system and getting into trouble with the staff. Rick played jokes on people and games like "Spray the guy in the bathroom stall with the fire house" and "Pee in the Tea"—Don't ask. Rick spent most of his senior year serving a punishment for leaving the dorm after curfew to get pancakes. He wasn't getting beer, girls, or engaging in some corrupt activity; just pancakes. They should have excommunicated him. Rick and I graduated together in 1993. Rick's grades put him in the middle of the pack at graduation. As for me, if it wasn't for my good friend Davon, I would've been the dumbest person in my class. In all seriousness, I am sure that I graduated second from last in my class. Again, Roanoke is a small school and it's always nice to tell people that I graduated twenty-fifth in my class, I just never tell them that there were only twenty-six of us that walked the stage.

Rick has been in ministry ever since graduation. He has a natural rapport with people, he's fun to be around and kids love him. A while ago, we received news that one of our classmates had committed criminal offenses while serving as a youth minister. Despite being academically sound (and a truly wonderful friend to me), he ended up doing time in prison. Rick said, "It's weird how so many really good guys didn't turn out and how some that the college deemed as 'problems' are still doing it (ministry)." The lesson learned is that regardless of educational prowess, or lack thereof; we're all capable of being servants. No one should be discounted or think themselves inadequate because they don't fit the mold or have a college education. Compared to godliness, humble availability and desire, knowledge is worthless in the arena of service. The best-case scenario is when a person allows those traits to compliment each other.

In some ways, I guess I thought that when I left school with my Bachelor's degree that ministry opportunities were just going to fall into my lap. Maybe I thought that I had earned something (other than the degree I received for completing my class requirements). Being a college graduate is something to be grateful for and proud of, it isn't a license for arrogance or an exemption from serving. My admiration for the people I most respect has nothing to do with the papers that hang on their office walls. My esteem is earned when I see someone helping someone else. Givers inspire me (and I'm not speaking financially) not takers. People who devote their lives to making other people happy before they are concerned about themselves are awesome. The father of four who works overtime so that his daughters can take a dance class is admirable. The people that give up their Saturday night bowling league to clean the church building the night before service are admirable. There are missionaries who could be working in high profile churches making a generous living here in America, who, instead, are living in poverty in West Africa pursuing wild and vile souls with the message of Jesus. I know many people who put their families, their churches and their God before themselves. They will earn something greater than a degree, a desk or the respect of those around them; they will earn a place for their names in the Book of Life.

One of my favorite movies is "Saving Private Ryan." In the movie, Tom Hanks stars as Captain John Miller, who leads a small group of soldiers into hostile territory on a mission to rescue a young soldier, Private James Ryan. Private Ryan's three other brothers die, almost simultaneously, in World War II. The soldiers in Captain Miller's group fall one by one during this rescue until there are only a couple of soldiers left to protect Private Ryan. In one of the closing scenes, Captain Miller is gunned down just as Private Ryan reaches safety. As he sits on a bridge dying, Captain Miller pulls Ryan close and says, "Earn this. Earn it." In essence, Captain Miller was saying, "I died saving you. Make your life count. Make my sacrifice worth it." Even though I love the movie, it actually shows a poor picture of grace. We can't earn Christ's sacrifice; if we could, it wouldn't be grace anymore. Jesus Christ laid down his life. He left heaven to enter a hostile environment and his mission was to save us. He died that we would reach safety. We could never earn or repay his sacrifice; we didn't deserve it. However, at the very least, our gratitude should drive us to make our lives count. What we can do in response to grace, is respond to it by giving ourselves as a gift of love. Because we are so deeply loved, we should want to love in return. Paul's thought was, *"the love of Christ compels me."* We should be willing to lay down our lives as a sacrifice to Christ and his children.

I have always loved the song lyrics that my friend Jay (my former youth minister from Son's Up) wrote for a musical called "Dead Serious About Life":

"After all you've done for me, I've responded selfishly
Here I am, so ashamed, tell me what to do
Try me now, show me how
Can I be used some way, somehow?
All I ask is make my life count for you"

The idea of sacrifice isn't a popular one in our society. We exalt the guy who hits homeruns and forget about the guy who moves the winning run into scoring position with a bunt. We want ripped abs from a seven minute, twice-a-month workout. We expect to win wars without the first casualty. Sacrifice is not a glamorous virtue. Rare in our time is the man who lay down his life for the cause of others. It was inspiring to see fire fighters rush into the flaming, crumbling towers of the World Trade Center during one of the worst tragedies in our nations history. Those men and women were more concerned about those who were inside the towers than in their own wellbeing. Many volunteers died that day. Those Americans understood sacrifice. Pro football player Pat Tillman left the football field and millions of dollars on the table of the Arizona Cardinals to serve his country. That decision ultimately cost him his life on the battlefield. Apparently, Pat Tillman understood sacrifice. Jesus, himself, said in John 15:13, *"Greater love has no one than this, that he lay down his life for his friends."* He later proved his belief in that statement by going to Calvary for the sins of the world. Jesus understood, preached and modeled service and sacrifice.

When I was a teenager, I watched a catastrophe take place on television. Growing up near Washington D.C., the Air Florida crash on Wednesday, January 13, 1982 was picked up by all of our local television stations and the rescue of several passengers was covered live in shocking and disturbing fashion. A major snowstorm was covering the D.C. area that day with considerable accumulation. The plane had taken off from nearby Washington National Airport, and due to wing icing and pilot error, the aircraft lost altitude and crashed into the 14th Street Bridge and the Potomac River less than a mile from the airport. There were only five survivors out of 79 people. The aircraft, a Boeing 737, descended nose-high and tail-low and struck the Rochambeau Bridge, hit seven vehicles, killed four motorists, injured four more and went into the frozen river between the Rochambeau Bridge and the express span. The aircraft shattered the surface ice, and broke into multiple large pieces, which quickly sank into the river. There were 78 fatalities.

The only five survivors were pulled from the frigid waters of the Potomac. A helicopter hovered above the snow-blanketed river and dropped a lifeline towards the survivors. These six people were clinging to a portion of the downed plane that stuck up out of the water. I remember watching one man in the water catching the lifeline and handing it to the person next to him. The chopper would then drag the person to the riverbank where numerous others had scaled down to help. The survivors were up to their necks in water that was unfathomably cold. Each time the lifeline came back to the wreckage, the same man handed it off. I actually remember asking my Grandmother, "Why doesn't that guy go?" It seemed to take a while for him to get the rescue line to his fellow survivors. Finally, there were only three people left, the man and two women. The line returned to the wreckage where the man, now barely visible, handed off again. As they pulled the one lady to safety, the other tried to swim away. She was in shock. She made it about half way and then began to fail. As her expression went blank, the lifeline dropped in her area. She couldn't grab it. Just as she was going under, a couple of the people on the bank jumped in a pulled her to safety. When the chopper went back to get the last man, he was gone. His name was Arland D. Williams, Jr.

"He was about 50 years old, one of half a dozen survivors clinging to twisted wreckage bobbing in the icy Potomac when the first helicopter arrived. To the copter's two-man Park Police crew, he seemed the most alert. Life vests were dropped, then a flotation ball. The man passed them to the others. On two occasions, the crew recalled last night, he handed away a lifeline from the hovering machine that could have dragged him to safety. The helicopter crew—who rescued five people, the only persons who survived from the jetliner—lifted a woman to the riverbank, then dragged three more persons across the ice to safety. Then the life line saved a woman who was trying to swim away from the sinking wreckage, and the helicopter pilot, Donald W. Usher, returned to the scene, but the man was gone."—from "A Hero—Passenger Aids Others, Then Dies", The Washington Post, January 14, 1982. The Rochambeau Bridge was later renamed the Arland D. Williams, Jr. Memorial Bridge. Arland D. Williams, Jr. understood service and sacrifice.

When my wife and I moved to Nashville in 2002, we only knew a couple of guys that I had recorded a comedy CD with the year before. One of those guys, Peter Vaque, modeled the true meaning of servant almost immediately after we arrived in Music City. Knowing that I was just starting out in a new ministry, Peter offered me some part time work with his company. His company sold and installed sound systems and lighting in every type of building imaginable. We weren't in Tennessee two days when I agreed to drive to Tampa to help him with a church install. We drove through the night and told the church that we would be there by 10 a.m. We took turns driving and I happened to be behind the wheel at 4:30 in the morning as we crossed the Florida state line and came up on a terrible accident. There were vehicles spun and wrecked seemingly everywhere and debris covered the road. In the midst of this bedlam, in the middle of highway 75, was a boat that had come off its hitch and flipped up on its side. People were running in the middle of the road, cars were running off the road, it was chaos. One man was out of his vehicle running towards oncoming traffic waiving his arms in attempts to alert all to the presence of an accident. Somehow I maneuvered Peter's van through the many obstacles and off to the side of an exit ramp. During the next hour, Peter showed me a level of service (and heroism) that many people never have the privilege of witnessing in their lifetime.

With an amazed expression and sweat on his brow, Peter thanked me for driving us through the accident safely and then jumped out of the van. He began directing me to his first aid kit and towels as he grabbed flashlights and bottles of water. Thirty seconds later, I found myself sprinting down the ramp with an arm full of supplies, trying to keep up with Peter. Despite living in a lawsuit happy world, Peter jumped over the guardrail and made his way toward a van that had rolled in the accident. As I approached the van, there were about forty people standing off to the side, seemingly frozen in place. As one little girl was watching and saying, "Mommy, mommy," Peter was helping a woman climb out of the top of the van. She jumped down with Peter's help and the little girl grabbed her around the waist and started to cry. The mother was in shock. With tiny spots of blood splattered on her face, she began talking about Disney and the weather and what time they would arrive at the park. I handed them both a towel and turned my attention back to the van. Peter was now on top of the van shining his flashlight down inside. The father was inside pinned by one of the seats. He said he was okay, just stuck, as was another lady (possibly an Aunt). When Peter realized they were okay, he asked, "Is everyone else out?" The father responded, "My boy is in the back."

Peter jumped down off the van and hurried to the back as I followed. When he opened the door, I knew immediately that something was terribly wrong. Peter looked onto the side of the road and yelled, "Is anyone here medically trained?" Unbelievably, two women raised their hands, each saying, "I'm a nurse." Peter implored them, "I need your help!" He told me to lay a couple of towels down on the highway as he started into the back of the van to grab the motionless body of a young boy. I would guess that he was ten or eleven years old, it was impossible to tell from what was left of him. Apparently, he had fallen asleep on a bed in the back of the van and wasn't wearing a seat belt. When the van rolled, the back glass busted. As the van slid on its side, the boy dragged on the pavement. To avoid the gory details, let's just say that the boy was suffering from massive head trauma and bleeding profusely. As he squeezed Peter's hand, I remember thinking, "How is he still alive?" Peter told the two nurses, "We have to move his head to the side; he's choking on his own blood." They agreed and proceeded to tilt his head to the side. Just then, a car came flying through the accident scene almost hitting Peter and one of the nurses. I handed them my towels and stepped back, urging others to do the same.

Helicopters and rescue units converged on the scene as the father yelled, "Where's my boy? How is my boy?" I asked one of the paramedics if there was any chance he might live, but in the middle of my question, she closed her eyes and shook her head, "No." Peter continued to hold the boys hand and wiped his face until the medics arrived. Then, with a face full of tears, he joined me on the side of the road. For a minute as I looked up at Peter, I forgot the accident and all that was happening around me; I was in awe. From the minute, we stopped our van, Peter turned away all concern for his own apprehensions, legal implications as well as his own safety and life, and turned his focus to serving a family he had never even seen before. It was heroic on so many levels. Peter earned my respect and admiration for life that morning. If the boy did survive, he would have Peter to thank for his life. Peter doesn't have a degree in Theology, nor is he a paid staff member of his church; He's just a person like anyone else. They say that adversity reveals character. Peter proved to be, in the most adverse situation, a servant of men.

Albert Schweitzer once wisely stated, "I don't know what your destiny will be, but one thing I know: The ones among you who will be really happy are those who have sought and found how to serve." A beautiful moment in our lives is when we experience the gratification that service produces. During my tenure in the Tampa area, I met a man named Charles. Charles was an older man, one of the oldest that attended our church. Charles was a tall, somewhat intimidating to look at, white-haired gentleman who proved to be just that. The first time you met Charles you discovered a soft spoken, pleasant and gentle man. He loved traditional hymns but once publicly acknowledged his appreciation for the modern worship that was "winning the young families" at our very young congregation. He was a good family man and a time honored Christian soldier in my eyes. One day after service, Charles stood and announced that his doctors had told him that he had cancer and very little time left on this earth. He stood, with tears in his eyes, and urged everyone present to quit smoking cigarettes. His doctors had told him they were the direct cause of his sickness. The announcement came as a shock to most and it wasn't long after, that Charles began to fade fast. When his hospice care ended, he and his wife requested that members of the church help provide care in his final days. Having never watched a man die before, I was a bit apprehensive when my shift came around. It was during those three eight-hour shifts that week that I learned this; there is no greater call than to serve someone in need.

Charles was a big man. He stood about 6'3 and even though his weight went down in the final weeks, Charles was heavy. During my second shift, he had to go to the bathroom. While he could hardly speak, he managed to whisper and point in a manner that I understood what he needed. I slowly helped him get sideways on the bed. He was sweating profusely. Just as I attempted to lift him a second time, I caught a glimpse of him looking at me. He seemed very humiliated. I recognized the shame that he must have been feeling, having his youth minister from church, lift him out of bed to use the bathroom. God's presence filled the room and I have never felt a greater sense of purpose and compassion in my life. I pulled his neck close to mine and hugged him. The words that came next were not scholarly or of intellectual counsel, they were my heart. "It's cool Charles, you know ... it's alright," I said to him as he cried. He squeezed my neck for what seemed like ten minutes. To this day, I have never known a more genuine and honest feeling in my life. It was the most rewarding moment in the history of my ministry.

Service impacts lives. Mother Theresa told us that God comes to us through suffering human beings. We can't all be Mother Theresa's but we each possess inner strengths and talents given to us so we can share them to others. Recent studies suggest that the benefits of serving others extend far beyond what we can do for others. Research suggests serving others can actually have a physical impact on your health. They call it "the helper's high," and it may even have a positive effect on the immune system. For instance, a study by the University of Michigan showed that life expectancy increases for people who volunteer (a 250 percent increase for men in the study). A study of Japanese elderly found that, regardless of gender, those who provide assistance to others rated their health more favorably compared with older adults who were less involved in their communities. More studies at Yale, Johns Hopkins, the University of California, the National Institute of Mental Health and Ohio State University support similar findings. We all possess a deep need to make a difference in the lives of others and serving teaches us that our lives have meaning. We raise ourselves to a purpose beyond our own immediate needs. Maya Angelou once said, "If you find it in your heart to care for somebody else, you will have succeeded." Nothing could be truer.

A short time after Hurricane Katrina devastated the southeastern part of the country, I had an opportunity to help with the cleanup effort in the small coastal town of Pass Christian, Mississippi with Campus Crusade for Christ. Our church sent all of our members an email asking for volunteers. My wife, Laura, and I prayed about it and decided that I should go. We called, they were delighted and then they sent us some information and waivers to sign. Call me crazy but I usually become somewhat nervous when I see words like hepatitis, disease, accident and death. I tend to get a bit concerned when reading phrases like "exposure to dead persons," "toxic environmental conditions" and "emotionally disturbing conditions or persons." After reading all of the above and more, I began to wonder ... and sweat. What if something bad happened to me? What if I brought back some type of disease? What if I didn't come back? As time passed, the possible hazards and potential disasters grew in possibility and drama. All joking aside, we really did weigh the possibilities of something going wrong.

After weeding through the excuses and considering the issue at hand, we believed that God wanted me to go on the trip. A few days earlier, as I watched the coverage in New Orleans, I had said to Laura, "I wish I could help." God answers prayer and wishes too sometimes. We filled out the paper work, signed the "Death Papers" and Laura packed my things. The emails they sent us said that we would be cutting down trees, digging mud out of people's homes and moving damaged furniture. I know about as much about chainsaws and tractors as Al Gore knows about inventing the Internet and, despite my athletic background, when it comes to brute strength, I am more like Olive Oyl than Popeye. Their emails explained that we would endure extreme physical labor so I was slightly apprehensive about what the days would be like. I was to ride down with the guy who was transporting a tractor. He pulled up to the church office in an old beat up pickup truck that looked like it had seen it's share of wars. There was tobacco juice and spit sprayed all over the dashboard. He introduced himself with a firm handshake. Rob looked like the guy who played high school football and belonged to the FFA. He said, "I hope speed doesn't make you nervous, because I drive like a maniac." I laughed and told him that I didn't mind a bit. I didn't know Rob. I was nervous.

During the eight-hour drive, I got to know Rob. The old saying about judging a book by the cover is true. Rob was a nurse, which immediately made me feel a little better about any injuries I might suffer. As we drove down the highway, he told me about his job. He worked in the O.R. and had several stories about what happens when things go wrong. We talked about his job for a couple of hours and I was fascinated. From his stories and his willingness to be on the trip, I knew that he was a person who genuinely wanted to help others. As we continued talking, we both expressed our curiosities regarding the conditions and work we were about to do. About two hundred miles north of our destination we began to notice trees down on both sides of the highway but we had no idea what we were about to see as we approached Gulfport, Mississippi. Aside from the trees, we began to notice subtle differences at first. Highway signs were down, a mangled golden arch over a McDonalds, hotel and restaurant signs smashed or completely gone. Many closed businesses displayed signs saying things like, "We'll be back." As we entered into Gulfport, we began seeing military vehicles. When we arrived on the shores, we were completely stunned. The smell was horrendous and the view was even more unbelievable. We saw a barge about three hundred yards in on the shore. We didn't see damaged houses as much as we saw piles of lumber, bricks and tree braches piled up on flattened lots. Most lots had cardboard signs on them, that displayed the owners last name, address and phrases like, "All accounted for," and "We're all o.k." There were crushed vehicles up and down the beaches along with other debris like refrigerators, computers and TV's. There was a boat in the middle of the road, giant sinkholes in the pavement every fifty yards or so and a church lying on its side. One pile of rubble bore a small Waffle House sign that said, "We will rebuild." Eventually we stopped at a military checkpoint as we journeyed west. We told them that we were going to Pass Christian and the guard said, "Oh yeah, it's really bad over there." I thought, "What could be worse than complete annihilation?"

In order to enter most of the beach, a military pass was required. Most roads were closed so we took detours and side streets towards our destination. Crime had been rampant. There were papers stapled to anything that still stood that encouraged folks to only hire reputable contractors. The signs read, "Don't Get Scammed. Don't be a victim of Non-licensed contractors." I sat in the passenger seat, mouth agape, considering the ramifications of these unthinkable subplots of the tragedy. Along the way, we saw guys sitting in lawn chairs in front of their properties holding shotguns. There were more signs and words spray-painted on sheets of plywood that read, "You Loot, We Shoot," "Go Ahead, Make My Day," and "You'll Never Take Me Alive." I had never seen anything like it. We arrived in Pass Christian, located our camp and set up tents outside of Trinity Episcopal Church. This once beautiful and time-honored structure had been gutted by a 42-foot storm surge that left only the steeple and a few supporting beams standing. It looked like an old camp pavilion. I called Laura to tell her that we made it and what I was seeing. When she asked me what it was like, I said, "This is the closest thing I can imagine to walking the streets of Nagasaki or Hiroshima after the atomic bombs went off."

That night I met the rest of our team. Our work force was comprised of a comedian, a nurse, a lady who owned a farm, two teenaged boys, a wealthy marketing executive and two of his employees. The seven castaways on Gilligan's Island would probably be better suited for helping the people of Pass Christian. That was what I found remarkable; we had eight very different individuals with no skills or expertise that would better enable us to help. Our group was simply willing to be there. A few days before the trip, my father told me, "You're doing a great thing son. Not everyone can go help." I understood what he meant, however, as I thought about it more and more, I disagreed. I think anyone who really wants to help others, finds the time, means or way to do so. I have made excuses my entire life as to why I can't do this or that, why I can't give more and how I am too busy to be part of certain things. In this case, I made the right choice and I was glad I was there. Looking around the camp, I saw countless college students who had come from Indiana, Pennsylvania and all over the country. There were many stunned expressions, concern, shock and fear. Neal Maxwell once said, "Don't fear, just live right." That's what these people were doing: The right thing.

The first morning we got up around 5:30 a.m. and went to the tents where they were serving breakfast. As we tried to wake up, an old man sat down at the end of our table. His hat bore the words "Veteran of the Korean War." He had the look of a man who had just been through another. He told us that this breakfast was more like his lunch. When we asked him what he meant he explained that he was working on his inland home. He stayed with family thirty minutes north and he would drive in to Pass Christian around 1 o'clock a.m. each day and work until 10 a.m. Then he would leave and sleep through the day. "The heat and humidity here is something like you ain't never had," he said to me in a rusty Cajun voice. We were about to learn that lesson the hard way. Our first job was to clean up an old cemetery behind the church. It was a large graveyard that had been there a while that was almost completely covered with shingles, boards, downed trees, trash and parts of destroyed vehicles. There was a semi turned upside down that was jammed into the side of a tree. It was a cluttered pile of devastation. Our team and about a hundred college students went to work on it.

By 10 a.m. it felt like it was afternoon. Our group was sweating it out in the middle of the cemetery, cutting up a couple of huge fallen trees and carrying away the pieces. Sweat seeped down my forehead. The heat was so intense I felt as though I could feel my heart beating inside my head. Sawdust kept getting in our eyes. At some point, we started pulling out larger, longer, heavier parts. I pulled one section from the pile and threw it up on my back. Some jagged bark dug into my back and I thought, "Man, I'm getting too old for this." As I pulled it through the rubble, my mind traveled far away from the gulf shore. At the risk of over dramatizing the strength it took to carry this section of tree, I thought, "I could not imagine being crucified." Jesus carried much heavier tree pieces up a long, steep hill just so that a few guys could nail him to it. The rough spots of the cross dug into his back, just after being gashed forty times with a cat-o-nine tails. I thought to myself, "No matter how bad it gets today, it could always be much, much worse." We finished our duties in the graveyard, ate lunch and got our shots for tetanus and hepatitis (the Red Cross was making it available). Then we went to a few houses in the community that were still standing to do various chores. That's when the heat really kicked in. In the five years I lived in Florida I never experienced heat like the blistering temperatures in Pass Christian. After an hour I developed a headache so bad, I could barely stand. At one point, I felt as though my brain was oozing out of my ears. The people, their faces and their expressions were the only things that kept me on my feet and moving. Each place we went to, we were welcomed warmly and thanked repeatedly. Sometimes the thanks came with hugs and tears. Every person we met had a story. Every few minutes I thought about my family, my home, my many blessings and how grateful I was to have them all.

Upon returning home, I barely managed to get myself up my stairs to the front porch. The three most important people in my world, Laura, Brooklyn and Katie, (Adrienne wasn't born yet) were there to greet me. I was glad to be home but just as grateful to have been to Pass Christian. Five minutes after I got home, I knew I was changed. I went to the fridge and before I could open it, I found myself off to the side in my laundry room, with tears running down my face, remembering those families with coolers in their homes. They had no power and therefore had no fridge so they would go to shelters or inland far enough to get a bag of ice and supplies to bring home every day. I love food but I never thought I would get emotional over a refrigerator. We are a truly fortunate people and most of us don't even realize it. Yes, we have refrigerators but most of us also have much more to appreciate. We should be thankful for everything from our bodies, to our minds to our health. We should be thankful for things like rain, music, family, friends and hobbies. I once heard someone say, "If you got a belly button on your body, then you owe somebody somewhere something." It's true; we all should be thankful.

Think about your life for a few minutes and your mind should be able to produce countless blessings regardless of your overall life fortunes or mishaps. Recently, I talked to a guy who shared with me all of his life frustrations, expressed his anger about his lack of breaks and even went to the "where's God?" and "Life isn't fair" cards. "Doesn't He know I have needs?" the man said. I said, "Needs? How many meals have you missed this week? Will you be able to go home tonight? Will you go there in your own car? Are you wearing socks and drawers?" Obviously not everyone could answer, "yes," to all of those questions, but I knew he could. "Well, yeah, but I want more," he said. I told him that there is a big difference between wants and needs. "Beyond all that," I said, "go home tonight and look in on your daughter as she sleeps, then come tell me that God hasn't taken great care of your needs and much, much more." This guy knows the Bible. He knew, deep down, that God has and does provide. The truth is that God is crazy about us. He loved us enough to sacrifice his Son to cover our sins. That being true, isn't it logical to conclude that he cares about our needs? Jesus speaks to the same type of pessimists in Matthew 6: 25–34; *"For this reason I say to you, do not be worried about your life, as to what you will eat or what you will drink; nor for your body, as to what you will put on. Is not life more than food, and the body more than clothing? Look at the birds of the air, that they do not sow, nor reap nor gather into barns, and yet your heavenly Father feeds them. Are you not worth much more than they? And who of you by being worried can add a single hour to his life? And why are you worried about clothing? Observe how the lilies of the field grow; they do not toil nor do they spin; yet I say to you that not even Solomon in all his glory clothed himself like one of these. But if God so clothes the grass of the field, which is alive today and tomorrow is thrown into the furnace, will He not much more clothe you? You of little faith! Do not worry then, saying, 'What will we eat?' or 'What will we drink?' or 'What will we wear for clothing?' For the Gentiles eagerly seek all these things; for your heavenly Father knows that you need all these things. But seek first His kingdom and His righteousness, and all these things will be added to you. So do not worry about tomorrow; for tomorrow will care for itself. Each day has enough trouble of its own."* I heard a minister once explain to his congregation that he is thankful for the many birds he sees while going in and out of various places when he runs his everyday errands. He explained, "Every time I see a bird fly by or hear one chirping, I'm reminded of how much God cares for me."

My first corporate job was with Bachrach menswear just outside of Washington D.C. The man that hired me, David Nichols, is a great leader and was an even better friend. David went on break with me one day. I had had a rough week, selling next to nothing as it were. I have always been transparent so everyone who saw me that day knew that I wasn't a happy camper. David took me into a bookstore in the Montgomery Mall and told me to sit down. He walked around the corner and returned shortly thereafter with a book in his hands. "Read this," he said and handed me a children's book. The book was "Did I ever tell you how lucky you are?" by Dr. Seuss. I had all of the classic Seuss books growing up but I didn't remember this one. I sat there reading this book, where an old and wise man tells a wacky story about countless unfortunates whose life circumstances were dreadful. I read page after page after page, enjoying it but wondering where it was going. Seuss, like so many great storytellers, had that extraordinary gift of pulling a deep, philosophical truth or message out of the simplest stories. I turned the last couple of pages and read this:

"Thank goodness for all the things you are not
Thank goodness you're not something someone forgot
And left all alone in some punkerish place
Like a rusty coat hanger in space
That's why I say, "Duckie, don't grumble, don't stew
Some critters are much, much, oh, ever so much, much
So muchly, much, much more unlucky than you."

I believe that when we are able to appreciate and understand how lucky we really are, service becomes something you truly want to do. The fulfillment that comes from bringing someone else happiness through our availability can be nearly inexpressible. Service impacts lives forever. Katrina helped me understand that in an entirely different light. Sometimes the servant changes more profoundly than the people he serves are. From seeing Peter's heroics on a Florida highway to being with Charles in his final hours to experiencing the aftermath of Katrina's devastation, I know that it is our humble availability and willingness to serve that ultimately are most important and fulfilling. We are truly most blessed when we put ourselves last and consider others first. Jesus said that serving is the way to greatness. In Matthew 20, Jesus says, *"It is not this way among you, but whoever wishes to become great among you shall be your servant, and whoever wishes to be first among you shall be your slave; just as the Son of Man did not come to be served, but to serve, and to give His life a ransom for many."* Born in a stable, a child of the lower class and a carpenter by trade, the King of Heaven came to touch lepers, wash feet and lay down his life for us with nails in his hands and feet. Jesus shows his disciples humility in the face of their arrogance. Pride is a sin that most easily besets us; it is sinful ambition to outdo others in pomp and grandeur. I once heard a speaker at a Salvation Army camp say that, "It was pride that turned angels into devils. But in humility, men can be turned into angels."

You may be asking yourself, "How can I experience serving in the fullest manner?" First, I would encourage you to make serving part of your daily life. Everyone should spend time volunteering to help others. So many people need your help. You may not see the significance of your willingness to be available. Little League coaches, Girl Scout leaders and piano teachers change the lives of many people. Have you ever visited an old folks home? Have you ever taken food or communion to a shut-in? Have you ever mowed their lawns or washed their cars? Things that seem trivial or small to us are often critical to those in need and usually remembered for life. Charles Shultz, the creator of Charlie Brown and Peanuts, once wrote out this philosophy in brilliant fashion:

Charles Schultz Philosophy

The following was the philosophy of Charles Schultz.

1. Name the five wealthiest people in the world.
2. Name the last five Heisman trophy winners.
3. Name the last five winners of the Miss America contest.
4. Name ten people who have won the Nobel or Pulitzer Prize.
5. Name the last five Academy Award winners for best actor and actress.
6. Name the last decade's worth of World Series winners.

How did you do? The point is, none of us remember the headliners of yesterday. These are no second-rate achievers. They are the best in their fields. Nevertheless, the applause dies. Awards tarnish. Achievements are forgotten. Accolades and certificates fade with their owners. Here's another quiz. See how you do on this one:

1. List a few teachers who aided your journey through school.
2. Name three friends who have helped you through a difficult time.
3. Name five people who have taught you something worthwhile.
4. Think of a few people who made you feel appreciated and special.
5. Think of five people whose company you enjoy.
6. Name half a dozen heroes whose stories have inspired you.

The lesson: The people who make a difference in your life are not the ones with the most credentials, the most money, or the most awards. They are the ones that care.

I know a tale of a Christian camp in Pennsylvania that inherited tens of millions of dollars by an old widow. Her husband, who was a steel mill innovator, died and she was lonely. Her family became complacent and visited her less and less. They, essentially, were just waiting for her to pass so that they could collect their fortunes. She began walking past this camp every morning for exercise. Every day the kids and people at the camp would smile, waive and talk to this lady. No one knew she was rich. When she died, she cited the friendliness of the children in her will and, in essence, wrote out her surviving family and left the camp her fortune. Words of encouragement, kind deeds and service are eternally essential for both the recipient and the servant. Sing in the choir, rake leaves, help someone in need, coach a team, be there for your child or spouse, … do something everyday. Make service a lifestyle. Make time to care.

Secondly, and equally important, don't neglect the other parts of your life—your family, your job, or your leisure time. This may seem to contradict the heart of service but there must be balance. Don't overload yourself with burdensome volunteer commitments. Moderation is the key to doing many things in life. Serving is no different; Let me explain. There are workaholics and there are "serve-aholics" as well. Of work, Charles Richard once said, "Don't be fooled by the calendar. There are only as many days in the year as you make use of. One man gets only a week's value out of a year while another man gets a full year's value out of a week." Having spent some time in the corporate world, I can tell you that just because you are a workaholic you are not necessarily gaining a "sustainable competitive advantage." We all have responsibility in numerous areas of life. If most of our energy is going into our work, we will certainly be borrowing from success in areas like family, health, spirituality and personal development. If you're working more than 60 hours a week, I'll bet you're sacrificing in other areas of your life.

God desires us to be servants, but certainly wishes our marriages to prosper and our families to flourish first. Your family should know that God is first in your life, but they should never feel like they are second to his church or its functions. It's hard to say "No" sometimes, but sometimes you have to. Objectively measure your time and your commitments and try to be fair and sensible. At the same time, don't wait until the end of the year to simply write a check. While that type of generosity is admirable and necessary, it won't change your life or touch its recipients on a personal level. Katrina would have never impacted my life had I only sent a check. Your church and community depend on your tithes and generous giving but they benefit even more from the donation of your time and active availability. Do something that has meaning for you. There is something essentially right about this balanced addition to our lives. You'll find making the time to serve others will provide you with more energy, instead of taking it away. As medical research is beginning to suggest, you're likely to live a longer and happier life as a result. Today is a great time to initiate this new practice in your life. Your life will never be the same once you have experienced the joy of helping others in a healthy manner. You can make a huge difference with the tiniest effort. In tennis, the game doesn't start until someone hits the ball. Grab your racquet; it's your serve.

3

"LEAP FROM THE BOAT, FOCUS, WALK ON WATER"

We all have weaknesses. You have weaknesses. Your mom has weaknesses and so does your dad. All of your heroes do, Donald Trump does, and the best football teams do too. The Death Star from Star Wars had one, Superman had one and the Titanic had one. Sampson had some, the apostle Paul had them and even King David had weaknesses. Your minister has them, your loved ones have them; we all do. Weaknesses are not bad things. Acknowledging that you have weaknesses is part of finding out where and how you fit in to God's plan. Andrew Murray wrote in his book, Abide in Christ, "As Christians, we often try to forget our weakness. God wants us to remember it. Too often, the Christian wants to conquer his weakness and to be freed from it. God wants us to rest and even rejoice in it. The Christian mourns over his weakness. Christ teaches his servant to say, "I take pleasure in infirmities; most gladly will I glory in my infirmities." The Christian thinks his weakness is his greatest hindrance in the life and service of God. God tells us that it is the secret of strength and success. It is our weakness, heartily accepted and continually realized, that gives us our claim and access to the strength of him who has said, "My strength is made perfect in weakness."

Paul says, in one of my favorite passages, 2 Corinthians 12: 9–10, *"My grace is sufficient for you, for my power is made perfect in weakness." Therefore, I will boast all the more gladly about my weaknesses, so that Christ's power may rest on me. That is why, for Christ's sake, I delight in weaknesses, in insults, in hardships, in persecutions, in difficulties. For when I am weak, then I am strong."* Our weaknesses are there to teach us to pray. When we acknowledge our weaknesses as we pray, his strength becomes perfect in our weakness and therefore his grace is manifested and magnified. When we realize that we are weak in ourselves, then we are strong in the grace of Jesus; when we feel that we are weak in ourselves, then we go to Christ, receive strength from him, and enjoy God's strength and grace.

By the time I began to realize the importance of acknowledging my weaknesses, I was serving as a located youth and worship minister outside of Tampa, Florida. I had been there for three years and had a successful ministry going. The church was growing, I enjoyed my life and service there but I felt somewhat unfulfilled. That emptiness first surfaced following a conversation with our most respected elder Ralph. Ralph was in his sixties, was retired and was the sacred cow among our leaders. Ralph was a visionary. He took me to breakfast every Wednesday morning to talk about his grandchildren, his golf game and his church. He was my eyes and ears. Ralph was a man of integrity and one of the most Christ-like persons I have ever met. Ralph pulled me aside one day and said, "Why are you here?" I wasn't sure what he was getting at. I responded profoundly, "What?" Ralph said, "Between you and me, I think you should start looking around for another opportunity." I thought I had done something wrong and that he was forewarning me of my eminent firing. Ralph assured me that I was doing a great job and told me, "I just want what is best for you. I want to see your potential realized. I don't know if you can accomplish that here. As an elder of this church, I'd like to see you stay here for twenty years but as your friend I'm telling you, if God puts that type of opportunity in front of you, you should go after it." Ralph was a great man and just as good a leader. Ralph would suffer a tear in his aorta a few weeks later and pass away.

As the church grew larger in number, the elders approached me with the news that they were going to hire a third staff member. They were going to have me choose which role I saw myself in, youth or worship. They also shared concerns that perhaps my heart wasn't completely devoted to the position anymore. They were simply observing a symptom of one of my weaknesses; I had grown complacent. Now I know that my complacency was born of a hollow faith. Let me explain. I believed in Christ as wholeheartedly as I could, I just struggled with the confidence that is required to do his will and trust him. I had accepted Christ, but I never fully trusted him. It was this lack of complete trust that prevented me from submitting to his will for my life and utilizing my gifts to their fullest measure. For years, I had heard God saying, "This is what I want you to do." Each time, however, I thought of every excuse, every potential problem and every reason why I should play it safe and do his will at a more convenient time later on.

When I was a young boy, my parents would take me on vacation to Ocean City, Maryland every year. However, when I was in fourth grade my parents announced that our family vacation, instead, would be in Myrtle Beach, South Carolina. They showed me the leaflet for the hotel where we would be staying. I looked through the brochure and immediately noticed a huge swimming pool, which was a major plus for me. The previous year, while at Ocean City, I had contracted the Chicken Pox and developed a fear of the ocean. The doctors told my folks that a boy with Chicken Pox shouldn't be out in the sun a lot. Given that advice, they thought it would be a good idea to take me to the movies. We went to see "Jaws." Suffice to say, a seven year-old wants nothing to do with the beach after seeing a large fish biting people in half if they dared to swim in the ocean. To this day, I have yet to receive a rational explanation for this completely outrageous parental decision. The pool at the Surf Rider was an Olympic sized pool complete with diving boards and the infamous 'deep end.' I had taken swimming lessons but still felt a bit uneasy swimming in 14 feet of water. My father kept telling me to use the diving board. I explained my hesitance and told him I would try later. This went on all week. Finally, one night when it was just he and I, my father put his hand on my shoulder and said, "Son, I think I know how to make this easier for you. I want to tell you something my father told me once." I left all apprehension behind anticipating a great story, some father-son bonding or some insight that would help me defeat this fear. We walked towards the side of the pool just to the side of the diving boards. As we walked across the painted words, "14 FT.", my father became very serious. "Son," he said staring down into the water with his hand still on my shoulder. "Look deep into this pool. Try to focus on the bottom." I concentrated on the shimmering image of the pool floor. "All you need ..." I suddenly felt the pool water smack my face. I felt a slight bit of pressure in my lower back where I began to realize my fathers other hand had pushed. My father had thrown me in and I was now going to die. As you can imagine my legs began running a hundred miles, an hour and my arms were flapping like a hummingbird with hyperactivity issues. I rose up out of the waters frantic, desperate and somewhat infuriated as well. I wasn't exactly singing the wondrous love of Jesus at that moment. As I grabbed the edge of the pool, I heard my father laughing. "All you need is a little push," he said.

My father taught me how to swim. That experience taught me something more important as I remember it now. Sometimes, all we need is a push. All we need is a small nudge. It only takes a kind word said to us, as Clyde had offered me when I was seven. Sometimes it only takes an encouragement, a small success or one answered prayer to cement our self-confidence as well as our trust in God. It is a natural tendency to fear things like deep water, extreme heights or darkness. The most successful people you know deal with fear and doubt in some form or another. It is difficult to achieve a trust in God that leads us to act on (what some call) blind faith. It can take place out of desperation. When we are in a situation that demands fast action, some of us demonstrate extreme measures of courage in unstable circumstances.

In the movie "Indiana Jones and The Last Crusade", Indiana experiences this. 'Indy' and his father are archeologists in search of the chalice that Christ used at the last supper. As the plot thickens, Indiana's father suffers a gunshot wound at the hands of the bad guys. Indy realizes that his dad has only a few minutes to live. He, then, faces with three tests that will lead him to the Holy Grail if he is successful or to certain death if he fails. After completing the first two success-fully, he walks out onto a ledge overlooking a seemingly bottomless chasm. He reads from his fathers' notes that the third test requires him to leap from one side of the canyon to the other. As he surveys this jump of what seems to be fifty yards or further, he realizes that it is a leap of faith. His father whispers, "It's a leap of faith. You must believe, boy." With his fathers' life being uncertain, Indiana Jones steps out, in faith, into the darkness.

While desperation can produce a stronger faith, I believe that acts of trust are more inspiring when taken out of sheer obedience. I have always been impressed with Jesus' influence on people in the Gospels. His persuasive personality alone is almost enough to convince one that he was more than just a good teacher or prophet. Throughout the Gospels, Jesus says these simple words *"Follow me."* Jesus says, *"Follow me,"* and turns fishermen, tax collectors and common men into evangelists, miracle workers and 'fishers of men.' Equally as impressive, is the faith of these men who dropped everything in order to follow him. It is easy for us to admire people who have made drastic lifestyle changes for the cause of Christ. But I find it far more admirable to hear the testimony of people who were brought up in the church, learned the ways of Christ, never got into trouble, loved their moms and dads, were married as a virgin and preach Christ with their life. How refreshing is it to meet people who have always done their best to obey God's Word? How inspiring to hear of a love for Christ that leads to a lifetime of faithfulness? How awesome is it that 2,000 years after he originally said, *"Follow me,"* men still drop everything and do just that?

For some people, like me, it takes a track record. God has provided for me repeatedly to the point that I would have to be completely blind to not acknowledge it. While Mary believed that Jesus had risen the moment the angel told her, Thomas had to see and touch his open wounds in order to believe. I can look back on my life and see where the angels in heaven probably have referred to me as "Doubting Tony." You know my type; "Yes Lord, I'll give when I have more." "Lord, if you do this and this and this, then I'll do this for you." "God, if you just make everything easy and eliminate all manner of risk, I promise I will trust you." We have probably all gone through certain things and different times with this mindset, if not those very words. At one point or another, we all have lacked faith. In one circumstance or another, we have all experienced fear. In one situation or another, we have all shown a weakness in this area or another. Just remember, weaknesses are a part of everyone's life but God is in control.

Jesus did something once that addresses our lack of faith at its core. I am sure that more than one of the disciples, if not all of them, struggled with their faith the same way we do. Sure, they may have left everything to follow him, but that doesn't mean they didn't have second thoughts, concerns or questions at times. We actually see the disciples' phobias all throughout Jesus' ministry. In Matthew 8:23–27, Jesus makes the ultimate statement for all who are weak in the area of faith. *"When He got into the boat, His disciples followed Him. And behold, there arose a great storm on the sea, so that the boat was being covered with the waves; but Jesus Himself was asleep. And they came to Him and woke Him, saying, "Save us, Lord; we are perishing!" He said to them, "Why are you afraid, you men of little faith?" Then He got up and rebuked the winds and the sea, and it became perfectly calm. The men were amazed, and said, "What kind of a man is this, that even the winds and the sea obey Him?"* Notice the reaction of the disciples. It's as if they were surprised. They magnify their lack of faith with a statement of doubt even after Christ proved his complete control, even control over Mother Nature. We do the same thing! We wait until the storm is upon us, pray diligently, worry and then are shocked when we receive answers to our prayers. Nevertheless, as evident in this story, man's extremity is God's opportunity. When we are at our most desperate hour God always seems to provide for us. Anyone who sails with Christ in this life must expect storms. Even people who have great faith are often weak in it. Thankfully, storms of doubt and fear can end in a wonderful calm. If Jesus can calm Mother Nature, he can surely manage the worst weather that life brings our way. I still have to remind myself of this, and remember this story, several times on an average week. God is in control.

The elders of our church wanted to know what my intentions were. My decision would be the first step towards the pursuit of new staff but I wasn't sure what to do. Initially I had accepted the position to be the worship leader. I thoroughly enjoyed that part of my life. I had developed a great relationship with the singers and musicians and looked forward to the prayer and ministry that took place at our practices each week. At the same time, I loved my kids. We had nearly quadrupled in size during my tenure and I had really turned the corner of trust with them. We had entered into that point in youth ministry when kids come to you for more than the fun stuff, the free stuff or the face (surface) stuff. One night, while eating out at a Shlotsky's Deli, things became even more complicated. While at dinner, I got a call from a guy in Tennessee who wanted me to come provide comedy and to speak at a camp week that summer. I told him that I could only be gone a certain number of days because of my ministry in Tampa. I told him, "Maybe we can do it next year." I hung up and asked myself, "How many of these things do you turn down each month?" It had never occurred to me. Actually, it had, but acknowledging the amount of calls would mean having to seriously consider doing what God created me to do. I may have to think about releasing the comfort and security of my weekly paycheck from the church and trust God to provide for me and I didn't want to do that.

I requested a week off to get away and pray about where God wanted me, leading youth, leading worship or something else all together. The elders agreed and I went home to pack my things to get away for a week. When my suitcase was loaded, I sat down on the steps of my house and started praying. I doubt I have ever prayed longer in one sitting. I began to weed through all of my thoughts and feelings with God as the sounding board. I prayed for clarity, his will, the youth group, the gift of discernment and I prayed for the church. I prayed to do the right thing. I prayed, for the first time, "God, make this obvious to me." As I prayed, I felt an overwhelming presence upon me. I felt assured that God would take care of me and I knew that he was helping me decide. That first night of prayer at my home I sensed that God wanted me to do what he wanted. I knew what that meant and it flew in the face of ration. It wasn't safe. It was somewhat crazy. I headed to central Florida that night and prayed for the duration of the trip. God was saying, "Just do what I tell you." I was saying, "Are you sure?" I kept thinking he would say something different.

I stayed at a youth camp near Lake Wales in a staff apartment that was vacant. I was there alone at the camp because it was in its off-season. I spent my days praying, shooting basketball, reading, dabbling with my artwork and talking to ministers I most respected for their insight. It was a week full of self-evaluation and bearing my soul to God. I'd never prayed with such candor, never been more vulnerable and never been so frank with God. All week I prayed, "Make it obvious." All week he said, "Just do what I tell you" and all week I answered, "Are you sure?" This went on until the following Sunday morning. I sat alone by the lake, returned to my apartment at the camp and packed my things. I prayed, "God, I'm heading back to talk to my elders tonight, are you sure you want me to do this?" Suddenly it was quiet: very quiet. It was so quiet that I could barely stand it. I prayed, "If you want to say something else, now is the time!" Nothing. As God was silent, I was starting to sweat. Not because of what God told me all week, but because I was starting to face the reality that I was going to have to take a leap of faith (something I didn't have a ton of) and demonstrate a trust in God that I had previously been unwilling to risk. I was about to get married. I was going to quit my job. I was going to start a traveling ministry and move to a new location in the course of a few weeks. As I drove out of the camp I thought, "I am just 'slap nuts.' This is completely crazy. Is this really God? Or is it just me? Is it his will or mine?" Then it happened. I had prayed, "Make it obvious," remember? As I pulled out onto the main road, I noticed an old church with a marquee out front. As I approached it, I began to read the words that would reinforce my decision and change my life. The sign read;

"Leap from the boat
Focus
Walk on Water."

Leap from the boat, focus, and walk on water. It was tremendously profound to me. At the same time, it was sort of like something out of the Twilight Zone. Remembering the clarity I 'd prayed for, I thought, "What's next? Will I get a few miles down the road and find Jesus hitch-hiking with a similar message scribbled onto a large piece of cardboard?" This was astonishing to me. What more could he do? How much more plainly could his will been stated? Even for an atheist, this would be hard to dismiss as coincidence. God had answered my prayers more clearly than I ever expected. I was going to marry Laura, quit my job and start a new ministry in a new town. The weight of the world seemed to fall from my shoulders, knowing that I was doing the right thing.

When I break down that old church marquee, several thoughts come to mind:

"Leap from the boat"

My father spent two years in the Army in the late 1960's in Vietnam. If I had a time machine that would take me to any place and time in history, Vietnam in 1968 would be one of my last choices. Years ago I tossed around the idea of joining the military so I asked my father what he thought and what it would be like. Dad told me, "You better be ready to jump. When they tell you to do something, man, you'd better do it and do it fast!" I thought to myself, "What will I do if they tell me to leap out of an airplane or chopper?" I had visions of being tangled up in my parachute, not being able to open my parachute and, even better, forgetting my parachute. I envisioned my fall from above with the sound of a whistle in decrescendo as I watched my horrified, plummeting face turn into a little puff of smoke on the ground miles below (very similar to the Coyote in the Road Runner cartoons). It didn't take me long to decide I might not join the Army.

We all have or have had someone to answer to in life. At one point or another, each of us has had a boss, teacher, coach or some type of superior that we knew we would never want to cross or disappoint. My high school basketball coach was the kind of coach that pulled you out of the game each time you made a mistake. Usually, if that happened, he wouldn't put you back in until each of your other nine teammates made mistakes as well and he had no choice but to put you back in. Similarly, I had a college professor, Mr. Steere, who had a zero tolerance policy for any type of miscue in his classroom. While at RBC I traveled as a college recruiter. Coming home from Minnesota, I had to sleep in a high school gym because of blizzard-like conditions. I had a term paper due the next morning. The college vouched for me, as did things like the news. In fact, I had paid one of the school's secretaries to type my paper the week before (a common practice amongst we men who type like Neanderthals with one finger) so that it would be ready for me upon my return. Even after he knew all of these things, he deemed my work late, gave me a zero and failed me. It wasn't a personal thing either. Mr. Steere was, and is, someone with a great sense of humor, someone I have high respect for and someone I know I can call a friend. We got along great (with that one exception). Suffice to say, I did my best to never cross him again.

As a Christian, and as a sinner, I am glad that God doesn't have a zero tolerance policy for my mistakes. His grace and mercy are two things that I will never fully understand. What is even more difficult to understand is why I am sometimes so reluctant to do what he says. For me, when I am honest with myself, it comes down to faith (or lack thereof). When I know God wants me to do something and I don't respond, I can say, "Lord, I trust you" but what I am really saying is, "Lord, I don't trust you" with my actions.

In Matthew 14:25–33, Peter, literally, 'leaps from the boat.' To his credit, he does, but not for long. *"And early in the morning he came walking toward them on the sea. But when the disciples saw him walking on the sea, they were terrified, saying, "It is a ghost!" And they cried out in fear. But immediately Jesus spoke to them and said, "Take heart, it is I; do not be afraid." Peter answered him, "Lord, if it is you, command me to come to you on the water." He said, "Come." So Peter got out of the boat, started walking on the water, and came toward Jesus. But when he noticed the strong wind, he became frightened, and beginning to sink, he cried out, "Lord, save me!" Jesus immediately reached out his hand and caught him, saying to him, "You of little faith, why did you doubt?" When they got into the boat, the wind ceased. And those in the boat worshiped him, saying, "Truly you are the Son of God."* People always look bad at Peter in this story. Granted he could've asked safer things of Jesus. He could have said, "Lord, if it is you, may there be $100 in my left pocket," or "Lord, if it is you, ask everyone except me, to come to you on the water." Usually, people view Peter as a failure in this story. The way I see it, however, is that at least he did what Jesus told him to do. The only reason he failed was that he took his eyes off Jesus. The moment he stopped trusting, he was in trouble. Even more so than our bosses, coaches, spouses and superiors, God expects us to do what he says. I would have run into the stands and stolen a fan's hotdog if my basketball coach told me to. We must be ready to show an even more fanatical obedience to the God of all creation. He will never leave us, steer us in a harmful direction or ask anything of us that we can't handle with his help.

"Focus"

Focus is such an important element in any recipe for success, no matter what you're cooking. As a seven year-old rookie in the Federal Little League, my coach with Kiwanis stood behind me, with his arms around my shoulders and hands on my hands as I stood at the plate during batting practice. He began helping me swing the bat in the direction of the pitcher. "The key to batting," he said, "is focus. Wolf, never, never, never, take your eye off of the ball." A few minutes later, he stood beside me crouched to the side of second base where I was playing defense. As one of our coaches hit a slow ground ball in our direction, he waited until it bounced off my kneecap into the outfield and said, "Wolf!" I looked at his determined eyes through my own tears as alert as I could be. "The key to fielding is to never, never, never, take your eyes off of the ball." Over the course of my eight years in baseball, while I became a solid Colt League level player, it was my inability to focus that lead to more strikeouts, foul tips and mental and physical errors than I'd like to admit. At the same time, the ability to focus led several of my teammates to successful play at higher levels.

Focus is critical in everything from baseball to driving a car. Focus is central to being the best you can be at home, at work and in your ministry. One of the most irritating things in the world is when the focus on your camera is off. This is especially when you have small children. You spend so much time and effort getting them dressed, into the right position and getting them to smile. Then at just the right moment, you push the button and "Click!" The flash goes off, you gasp with hope and you anticipate seeing your child featured in magazines via your nearly professional, perfect shot. You go to the computer and download the shot only to discover the unthinkable. The smile was vintage, the composition is flawless and, yes, the focus was slightly off. The focus isn't far off; it's just barely off. The blur is slight yet it is just blurry enough to scrape its nails over your optical chalkboard. "Uuugghh! For the love of Minolta!" When our focus is even slightly off, our goals and objectives blur. Most cameras have a featured called "Auto Focus." This allows them to focus on their subjects in any and every situation. No matter if it is pitch black, if there is a blinding light, if it's foggy or if you are underwater—the Auto Focus kicks in and the result is most often beautiful. We, unfortunately, don't come with an Auto Focus feature. Webster defines focus as "concentrated effort or attention on a particular thing." Focus demands a great deal of self-discipline and requires us to set priorities.

In Luke 10, Jesus teaches another lesson in focus. I love this story because of its relevance for us. We are, largely, an undisciplined people. We often put the wrong things first. We focus on things that are actually somewhat trivial in the big picture. I recently talked to a guy who had watched some old home videos of himself and his daughter when she was very young. He said, "Man, I was a jerk." I asked what he meant. He continued, "I watch those old videos and see that I was so consumed with my daughter not doing this and not doing that, not saying this and not saying that. I must have verbally chastised her a hundred times, just on that one tape! It's a wonder she ever had any fun. I should've been more patient. I should've spent more time playing with her and less time correcting her." Many of us consider our jobs more important than our families. Maybe not with our mouths, but with our actions it's true. We say, "I need to get this done" and "I need to do that" when what we really need to do is dance and play house with our daughters. We say, "I need to put more time in at the office to get that promotion or raise," but what we really need to do is to take our spouses out on a date. We say, "I need some ME time," when what we really need to do is go see our folks and grandparents, see if they need anything. We say, "There aren't enough hours in the day" when God would be pleased with the progress of a few five minute prayers from us each day. We rush in and out of our rooms and homes, busy with so many 'important' things, while our spouses, kids and God sit waiting patiently for their turns. Sometimes they wait a long time and other times they wait a very long time.

More than you know, I understand the importance of our jobs, responsibilities and our "ME time." Those things require our focus and time. Our kids are only little for a few short years. Our spouses are not to be taken for granted. We only have our parents and grandparents for as long as God grants them breath. Moreover, God isn't there for us to approach on Sunday morning only; he desires an every day relationship with us. Think about it this way: How happy would your spouse be if you only talked to her a few seconds before an occasional meal? How much would your relationship prosper if you only spent five minutes together two or three times a week? How well could you get to know her if you only saw her on Christmas Eve, Easter and for an hour every nine or ten Sunday mornings? Who would describe those conditions as a focused, healthy relationship for a husband and wife or for a person and God for that matter? Focus makes us ask, "What is most important, really?"

Jesus understood the magnitude of focusing on the most important things. He realized the importance of spending time at his feet. Starting in Luke 10:38, *"As they continued their travel, Jesus entered a village. A woman by the name of Martha welcomed him and made him feel quite at home. She had a sister, Mary, who sat before the Master, hanging on every word he said. However, all she had to do in the kitchen pulled Martha away. Later, she stepped in, interrupting them. "Master, don't you care that my sister has abandoned the kitchen to me? Tell her to lend me a hand." The Master said, "Martha, dear Martha, you're fussing far too much and getting yourself worked up over nothing. One thing only is essential, and Mary has chosen it—it's the main course, and won't be taken from her."* Simply put, Jesus tells Martha, *"Mary is doing that which is most important."* If you ask yourself that question throughout the day ("Am I doing what is most important?"), without focus you're likely to answer "No" most of the time.

Prioritizing is the key to the realization of our focus. Recently I decided that my time on the road needed to decrease. I had one little girl, one on the way and a wife whose full-time job was being a stay home Mom. I didn't want to miss anything; not the first steps, not the first dance class, not the first game and not my wife's birthday or our anniversary or anything else either. I also needed good sound advice and direction for my ministry and how a decrease in travel dates would affect it. Laura and I turned to a professional company in North Carolina to help us determine what our goals were for our ministry as well as our family. After talking for just a few minutes, the lead consultant, Dan, asked, "What's most important to you?" We both looked at our eighteen-month old daughter and responded, "Our family." Dan said, "Let's start right there." For the next several hours, we developed a plan (and put it in writing) that would enable me to be home more and gone less. The remainder of our time was devoted to the vision of our ministry and some business related subjects. Laura and I were pleasantly surprised when we looked at my schedule eight months later and found that I was not only gone less, but I was gone less than we had written into our plan. To borrow a phrase from the company we hired, "It's been said that the definition of insanity is "Continuing to do the same things but expecting different results." Prioritizing enables us to develop some positive changes in our behavior and helps us to focus on that which is, in fact, most important. Not everyone who reads this book should go out and hire a company. Maybe not everyone should write your priorities down, though that does seem helpful to most people who are setting goals and clarifying their objectives. However, I would advise you to ask God for wisdom and to make the most vital things obvious. Ask him to help you focus on the things that are most important as you begin each day.

"Walk On Water"

When I hear the phrase 'walk on water', I immediately think of Jesus. The next thing I usually think about is extraordinary people whose stories are nearly unbelievable. Names like Helen Keller, Ludwig van Beethoven and Joni Erickson Tada come to mind. Suffice to say, tales of deaf, mute and blind teachers, deaf composers and paralyzed artists inspire us all. Wilma Rudolph also comes to mind. Her tale is an incredible testament to human will and determination. As a young girl, Wilma was tutored at home because she was crippled. Wilma was the 20th of 22 children in her family. Her parents were honest and hard working, but very poor. All of these obstacles never slowed Wilma down. By the time she reached high school, she became a basketball star and set state records for scoring and led her team to a state championship. Then she became a track star, going to her first Olympic games in 1956 at the age of 16. She won a bronze medal in the 4x4 relay. On September 7th, 1960, in Rome, Wilma became the first American woman to win three gold medals in the Olympics. She won the 100-meter dash, the 200-meter dash, and ran the anchor on the 400-meter relay team. Wilma was a champion who, just a few years before, couldn't even walk. Few people have a greater story than Wilma Rudolph does. When I hear the words, 'walk on water' these are the people I remember.

Then I think of Peter. Peter is the only other person in history who literally did walk on water. How amazing is that? A fisherman actually walked on the surface of the sea. Peter wasn't an Olympian or a magician. Aside from the fact that he spent three years with Jesus, Peter was as ordinary as you and I. You may be thinking, "Well, yeah, but Jesus made that happen." You would be half correct. Without faith, Peter wouldn't have even stepped out. Jesus, and Peters' faith in him, enabled this miraculous stroll to occur. However, doesn't God's word tell us that we have the same advantage? *"I can do all things through Christ who strengthens me."* Philippians tells us that we can do all things through Christ. Christ hears our prayers and knows we desire to be the best we can be for him. I believe that discernment comes from the Spirit regarding what we are supposed to do for God. Unfortunately, as I learned the hard way, until we believe that and trust in him enough to let him work on and in us, our ability to see that, can be somewhat clouded. In our apprehension, I'm sure that God must wonder, "You of little faith, why do you doubt?"

In my situation, I had lined up some reasonable and very valid excuses to explain to God why I wasn't doing his will. "We're about to get married. We're making decent money. We like it here in Florida. We don't even know anyone in Nashville. Maybe this church will eventually be where God wants me to be. Maybe this is my will, not his." What I was really saying was, "God, I don't think you can meet my needs. I doubt you will bless my new wife and I. I'm not convinced that you will pour out your blessings, even though you said you would." All the while God was probably wondering, "Why do you doubt?" I was 33 years old, an ordained and practicing minister yet faith, ironically, was my biggest weakness. God's word, however, encourages us in the midst of our shortcomings.

1 Cor. 12:9–10, "And He said to me, *My grace is sufficient for you, for My strength is made perfect in weakness. Therefore, most gladly I will rather boast in my infirmities, that the power of Christ may rest upon me. Therefore, I take pleasure in infirmities, in reproaches, in needs, in persecutions, in distresses, for Christ's sake. For when I am weak, then I am strong.*" Notice how Paul doesn't just say I get by or I take them one day at a time. Paul says I take pleasure in my weaknesses! When we are at our most transparent, our weaknesses should produce a sense of helplessness. Where do we always turn when we feel we have no place to go? We go to God, we ask him to supply our needs and then we are shocked when he provides.

It wasn't until Laura and I took this huge leap of faith (huge for us anyway) that we started seeing God show up repeatedly as we prayed. It was almost tickling to observe this. As I had heard so many people testify in years past, I began to see God answer prayer within the day and sometimes the hour. When times would get tough, we would sit down and say, "What are we going to do?" Then after wasting time thinking of new marketing ideas or coming up with numerous hairbrained remedies, one of us would say, "We're going to pray." We would pray and an hour or two later the phone would ring and someone would be inquiring about a program or speaking engagement. On numerous occasions that call would be followed by another within a few minutes. Can you say, "My cup 'runneth' over?" An unexpected check would show up. Someone would pay me double what I originally asked because we 'blessed' him or her with our ministry. God has always taken care of my needs, but his presence was never more obvious than when I took a step towards him in my own helplessness. I'll never physically walk on water, but I feel just as blessed to have walked towards him through the stormy forecasts that I have.

I was very scared and sometimes skeptical when I first arrived in Nashville. I wondered if God didn't want me to eventually go back into a located ministry and I wavered quite a bit in the early stages of my new vocation. At one point, I received a nice position with a church in Oklahoma. I went to the interview in an honest attempt to let God lead me. Laura and I prayed, "Make your will obvious to us" and he did. We headed home early the next day amidst a wave of red flags. The next weekend I was to perform at a huge Youth Conference. I was one of those late night options where you start performing at 11:30 at night and 14 people (out of 7,000) show up to watch. Laura and I walked around the next day and watched all the main sessions. There were thousands of people, light shows, pyrotechnics, live chickens, dancing girls—you name it, they had it. The poorly lit conference room that I had given my soul to the night before to the sound of scattered claps, grasshoppers and the janitors' vacuum cleaner was not encouraging. It was extremely embarrassing that my wife, Laura, had actually witnessed this debacle and I felt like an idiot afterwards thanking the 5 youth leaders, their spouses, my parents and their dog for coming.

As we left the next day, we got into our car and Laura turned to me and said, "You belong." I half expected her to follow that with, "on the Gong Show" or "in an insane asylum." I turned and said, "What?" "You belong," she said again with a big grin on her face. Now I was interested. "You don't just entertain, you have something to offer people. You can speak the truth and people feel good while you're doing it. God made you for this. This is where you belong." She went on to talk about how obvious God was making my place in the world. We prayed from St. Louis to Nashville. We came home, created some limited, but professional, promotional material and have not looked back since. I am so fortunate to have a wife who is, not only supportive, but both honest and encouraging as well.

Since laying aside my hesitance and apprehensions, God has blessed my ministry, business and life unlike ever before. Make no mistake it hasn't been easy. It has meant hard work, extended faith and sacrifice. Now let's talk about the most relevant and difficult part. Where do you fit into God's plan? God wants to use your strengths, work through you with your weakness and reach others with his perfect love. He has a plan for your life. Regardless of where you've been, what you've done, how tall or short you are, how you talk, how you walk, how much talent you do or don't have, he wants to work through you. It is, however, his plan. Many times, if not most, his plan is different from ours. Many people, selfishly, do their own will and attach God's name to it. That's not to say that we shouldn't do what we enjoy to accomplish his plan. Psalms 37:4 reads, *"Enjoy serving the Lord and He will give you what you want."* Finding where you fit does involve realizing what you enjoy, what you are passionate about and what fills you up. Finding your strengths is as important as accepting and acknowledging your weaknesses. In Romans 12:3, Paul says *"Have a sane estimate of your capabilities."* Be realistic and always ready to adapt. Your place is somewhere between your abilities and his plans. I thought I would be a musician. I played serious music that I had written and everyone laughed so I thought, "Why not give them what they want" and ultimately became a comedian. My message is still the same, it's just comes from a different pulpit now. Most of us start on one path and end up on a different path entirely.

For example, Babe Ruth is famous around the world as a great baseball player. Anyone who knows anything about baseball knows how Ruth hit 60 home runs in a season and over 700 homers in his career. The stories of his days as a Yankee and his love for kids are a dime a dozen. However many people, even good baseball fans, don't know that Ruth played for the Baltimore Orioles or that he started out as a pitcher. In fact, the Sultan of Swat was one of the best World Series pitchers of all time. Ruth, like so many people who are great at what they do, had to find himself.

George Herman Ruth was a mischievous young man. He skipped school, ran the streets and even committed petty crime. By age seven, he was already drinking, chewing tobacco and had become too difficult for his parents to deal with. There are many stories about Ruth's father beating him ruthlessly in an attempt to discipline him but to no avail. Ruth eventually wound up at St. Mary's Industrial School for Boys where his life was changed. The schools disciplinarian was a man named Brother Matthias. Brother Matthias helped Ruth turn his life around and introduced him to the game of baseball. Because of his "toughness", Babe became the team's catcher. He liked the position because he was involved in every play. One day, as his team was being pounded, Babe started mocking his own pitcher. Brother Matthias promptly switched Babe from catcher to pitcher to teach him a lesson. However, instead of getting his comeuppance, Babe shut the other team down. It was evident to Brother Matthias that Ruth was special. Ruth continued to pitch, eventually turning pro with the Baltimore Orioles. One day, while shagging fly balls in practice, a thought occurred to Ruth. "I'll win more games playing everyday in the outfield than I will pitching every fourth day," Ruth thought.

Ruth switched and the rest is baseball history. Babe Ruth had a career batting average of. 342, 714 homeruns and is still today one of the most celebrated players in the history of the game. Ruth was inducted into the Baseball Hall of Fame in 1936 after helping the Red Sox and Yankees win seven World Series titles. Of course he was also a perfect three wins and zero losses as a World Series pitcher, with an ERA of 0.87 including a 14-inning complete game victory over Brooklyn as a member of the Boston Red Sox. As great as Ruth was at pitching, he truly found himself the day he stepped into the batter's box with a menacing piece of lumber on an every day basis.

At a recent program in Florida, I saw an old friend who had previously watched me struggle in a ministry that really wasn't meant for me. She watched, nearly cringing for me, as I attempted (with a microscopic-sized faith) to figure out how God was going to use me. After the program, Anna Zickafoos approached me and said, "Looks like you've found your niche'." God constantly speaks to us through his people. He encouraged me as a child through the impact of Clyde, as a young man through the tutelage of Jay and confirmed me in my ministry as a middle-aged man through the words of an unlikely old friend. It took me nearly forty years but I had finally found myself. It is more apparent to me every day that getting to know yourself is a lifelong process. It doesn't come without heartbreak, mistakes and failures. Believe me, I have failed in every area in my life at one point or another. Babe Ruth, as great as he was, also struck out more times than any other player in baseball history. You will struggle at times, you'll have to fight and you'll wonder why bad things still happen to you now and again. You will also have to do many things along the way. Search. Acknowledge and embrace your weaknesses and strengths. Listen. Leap. Focus. Be open to his plan and develop the ability and willingness required to act on your faith. Be completely honest with yourself and with God as your quest for authenticity takes place.

4

"ESPECIALLY YOU"

Frank J Giblin II once said, "Be yourself, who else is better qualified?" As I began writing this book I thought, "Who am I to write a book?" I felt completely unfit, under-qualified and far too shallow to embark on such a project. I had many ideas and subjects that I considered from drama books to fictional murder mysteries. No, that isn't a typo … murder mysteries. I always enjoyed "Who done it?" type stories and TV shows as a kid. While I will completely deny it publicly, I have to admit, there was a time when I loved Nancy Drew and the Hardy Boys. Of course, that was a long time ago, I barely noticed that they recently released all of the episodes from season one featuring Pamela Sue Martin, Shaun Cassidy and Parker Stevenson on DVD. Anyway, I sought advice from peers, asked many questions, talked to authors and bought a few books to help me begin. However, suggestion number 78, shared by an old friend, really resonated with me. My friend said, "Write about what you know." That counsel came to me during a long tour. The busier my travel schedule the more I hear these types of questions; "How did you get started as a comedian?" "What advice would you give someone who is attempting to become a singer (or musician or entertainer or minister)?" "Where do you get your original material?" "Do you work at a church?" Armed with my friends' advice and the onslaught of similar questions, I decided to write about what I really knew about. I decided to write about how my experiences led me to the greatest purpose in life: how to be a servant. Moreover, I decided to write about how someone could use their unique abilities and God-given persona to impact others. I felt I could write about this confidently. As you continue to read, allow me to share one disclaimer. The stories, approach and avenues I have traveled may not be helpful to you. The way I handled certain situations may not be applicable according to your particular gifts or personality. My hope is to share with you, with a slightly different slant, information that has been life changing for me. That said I would encourage you in all facets of life, to be yourself.

Since childhood, I have always liked the different; not better, just different. My favorite singers, actors and athletes usually were the ones deemed unusual or 'unique' at the very least. Mark "The Bird" Fidrych was one of my favorite athletes of all-time. The ironic thing is that Mark Fidrych wasn't a great athlete. They called him "The Bird" because of his physical appearance. Fidrych looked a lot like the Sesame Street character "Big Bird." Fidrych was a pitcher for the Detroit Tigers for a little over four years. "The Bird" was my favorite player because of his behavior on the mound. He would talk to the baseball; I mean he would really talk, full-blown conversations, to the ball. He would scold the ball if it didn't go where he attempted to throw it and he would laugh with and massage the ball if it found the strike zone. Fidrych would throw back balls that "had hits in them," insisting they be removed from the game. Even though almost everyone loved him, more than a few people thought that there was a little something wrong with Mark Fidrych. On June 28, 1976, I was amazed as I watched him pitch against the New York Yankees in a nationally televised game on ABC. The Tigers won the game 5–1. After a game filled with "Bird" antics in which he and his team handily defeated the Yankees, Fidrych became an instant national celebrity. Unfortunately, a torn rotator cuff ended Mark's career in 1980. Mark Fidrych was different.

I grew up listening to Motown music. My father may be the only man in America who would watch Hee-Haw and Soul Train back-to-back. In the process, I came to like singers and groups like Stevie Wonder, the Jackson 5 and the late James Brown. James Brown, known by most as "The Godfather of Soul", would probably never have received a positive review from Simon Cowell. Brown's vocal performances included hundreds of different shouts, shrieks, screams, yells, screeches and howls that could frighten a banshee. I say that with the highest level of respect. James Brown was a three-figure hit-maker with 114 total entries on Billboard's R&B singles charts and 94 that made the Hot 100 singles chart. Seventeen of these hits reached number one. James Brown was different. Many of the top record makers of all-time would not consider themselves the greatest vocalists. From Willie Nelson to Bob Dylan to the Beatles, authenticity, not phenomenal singing, has been the vehicle to success.

God rarely uses the most educated, wealthiest, talented people to carry out his service. God specializes in underdogs. God didn't use the Heavyweight Champion Goliath; he used a young (and very small by comparison) David to become King and lead his people. David, to add to his resume, was also an adulterer and murderer. Still, the Bible calls David "a man after God's own heart." God called a murderer of Christians and persecutor of the faith when he used Paul to evangelize and write more than half of the New Testament. Jesus could have come to earth with uncountable riches, in a position of power but instead he was born in a barn to a low class family to become a carpenter. He could have come to kick butt and take names, like Judas and other revolutionaries and Zealots wished, but instead Jesus modeled servant hood, taught humility and built his ministry on love. Napoleon Bonaparte once said, "Alexander, Caesar, Charlemagne, and myself founded empires; but what foundation did we rest the creations of our genius? Upon force. Jesus Christ founded an empire upon love; and at this hour millions of men would die for him."

Consider the many people God used to do his will who were different. The first person that I think of is John the Baptist. Matthew 3:1–6 says, *"In those days John the Baptist came, preaching in the Desert of Judea and saying, "Repent, for the kingdom of heaven is near." This is he who was spoken of through the prophet Isaiah: "A voice of one calling in the desert, 'Prepare the way for the Lord, make straight paths for him.'"* John's clothes were made of camel's hair, and he had a leather belt around his waist. His food was locusts and wild honey. People went out to him from Jerusalem and all Judea and the whole region of the Jordan. Confessing their sins, they were baptized by him in the Jordan River." Years ago I performed outdoors at East Carolina University. As we did our sound check, a man jumped up on a picnic table and started screaming "Repent! Repent! You workers of iniquity! Turn or burn, you adulterous generation!" The man wore a bathrobe, briefs, a trucker hat and army boots. He carried a Bible that was bigger than he was, claimed that he had invented lunchmeat and threatened to light himself on fire. The police came and took him away. As crazy as he was, even he probably wouldn't have enjoyed John's locust and honey sandwiches. When I read Matthew and think of John the Baptist, I inevitably think of the lunatic I saw at ECU. John the Baptist was different for sure. His wardrobe was different, his diet was different and his message was different too. He was, however, the voice to help prepare the way for the messiah.

In June of 1987, I met an extraordinary man. While traveling with, the fore mentioned, "Son's Up" group from the beginning of June through the end of August. We started the summer with a two-week tour of the east coast with a full 40-man roster of teenaged singers, actors and light and sound guys. We performed at churches on most nights and, occasionally, we journeyed to camps or convention centers. One night we played at a small Christian camp in Mechanicsville, Virginia outside of Richmond. Oak Hill Christian Service Camp was one of the most pitiful facilities to ever host camp weeks for humans. Over the next few years, I found myself at this sub par, unsanitary campground more weeks than I would've liked. There are missionaries that wouldn't stay at this camp. The camp is located 57 miles into the woods, down a long, dusty lane, behind a wall of thousands of trees, just past a small creek, smack dab in the middle, of the middle, of nowhere. Several of the buildings wouldn't pass inspection if the government were ever aware of their existence. Don't get me wrong, a little Spackle, a few nails and some napalm and the place would be wonderful. Dilapidated structures, poisonous snakes, deadly insects and a guy that liked to wonder through the woods in a hockey mask were some of the perks that the camp never put on it's brochures. The camp mascot was a three-legged dog affectionately named "Tripod." The suggestions that the camp sat an old Civil War burial ground never surfaced in the local churches when it was time to sign kids up. However, the most bizarre thing about this camp was a young man named Mark Lukhard.

Mark sat in the front row during our performance. You couldn't miss him. He and his friend, Jeff, were about as hard to notice as a 500-pound senior citizen dancing around a water sprinkler in nothing but an oversized diaper. Mark and Jeff were dressed as if they just came off the set of Michael Jackson's "Beat It" video. Jeff wore an outfit that may have been designed by the Glad Trash bag people and jewelry rivaled only by Mr. T. His hair reminded me of something that would cause an argument between "Flock of Seagulls" and Don King. Mark was even more striking. Prince could have switched clothes with Mark and neither would have looked any different. Amidst a plethora of chains, studs and earrings, Mark's hair stood erect in every direction imaginable. You almost expected him to spew a "Cock-a-doodle-do" whenever he opened his beak. I thought to myself "This guy must be a huge Foghorn Leghorn fan." Mark and Jeff were different to say the very least.

Mark and Jeff laughed, clapped and danced throughout our show that night. I wasn't sure what they would think. They really enjoyed it. They congratulated us after the program and thanked us for coming. As we were tearing down our equipment and loading our bus, one of the camp staff approached us and said, "You guys are welcome to attend our campfire service. There's a guy speaking tonight that you really need to hear." We decided to attend and when we got to the campfire, the scene was typical. A couple of college students with a guitar and tambourine led the campers, mostly high school students, in singing songs of the "Kum bah yah" variety. What happened next, was far from typical.

Emerging from the surrounding woods came an ear-piercing chant. "Give me a J!" A voice shrieked to the hundred or so eager teens. They all responded with a roar that echoed off the trees, "J, you got your J, you got your J!" As expectations built to a frenzy the mantra continued to E, S, U and another S. Seconds later the name of Jesus was being bellowed out against the woods in perfect time like the chorus of "We Will Rock You" by Queen. Mark's silhouette came into view from the woods with energy unlike anything I had ever experienced. As he preached, he circled the campfire and the light began to strike his face as he turned. When he faced me, I saw an intensity that was both commanding and intimidating. Then, as he continued to walk around the fire, I saw his back, which made him appear to be a stalking shadow. This was the perfect contrasting stage for the young evangelist who, so passionately preached about light and darkness. As he continued to recite passage after passage without a Bible, words like 'Revolution', 'Uprising' and 'Eternal Hell' amplified with the same type of power and energy you would expect from an electric guitar at a rock concert. It was unbelievably electric. I watched in stunned silence as people began to come forward, bow, pray, and even leave weeping. Demons scattered from the fire into the blackness of the forest that night. Mark was the most authoritative speaker I had ever heard. The amazing thing, however, was while he preached a message filled with hellfire and brimstone, he didn't come across as hateful or judgmental. I felt as though he genuinely loved and cared about every person who listened including me. That night I not only witnessed twenty or so young people give their lives to Christ, I heard stories about how this was becoming a routine theme following Mark's sermons.

That summer, Mark and I became friends. He had become a fan of my music and comedy and I was amazed at what God was doing through his testimony. Mark had led a rough life leaving home at a young age in complete rebellion. He developed a talent for break dancing (and dancing in general) and for rapping, as hip-hop culture grew from its childhood in the 70's and into its young prime in the early 1980's. This would serve him as a virtual passport into places that pre-teens ordinarily and legally could not go. Mark began 'working' to liven the atmosphere and enhance the profits of many clubs in the Richmond, Virginia area. This is where Mark would meet Jeff, whose story was very much like Mark's story. Jeff left home to escape the Christian home that would not be a haven for the radical, counter-cultural person he was becoming. Mark and Jeff desired to fill their voids. Like many people, they were attempting to fill themselves via the talents God gave them instead of using God himself. Of course, the club scene brought with it "the life." Without specifics, Mark and Jeff found themselves in the middle of more fights, alcohol, girls and drugs then you can fathom. They were popular, independent, making money and living "the life," but something wasn't complete. At the core, there was something still unfulfilled. Imagine that.

In the summer of 1987, something happened. "We came to the Lord, and to our senses, as a result of Jeff's praying mom," Mark said in a recent interview. Jeff's mom was a devout Christian and a prayer warrior. She was worried for both her son and his friend. One day she got an idea. After many prayers and more tears she said, "I dare you two to go to Christian service camp this summer." Mark and Jeff must have both been thinking a collective, 'What?' At first, they thought she was kidding but she persisted. "I dare you two to go to camp." They laughed. They laughed for quite some time. They laughed, chuckled and even cackled a bit. They thought, 'Oh sure, we'll fit right in. Christians are sure to love guys with Mohawks, tattoos and piercings, gyrating around with a microphone in one hand and a forty-ounce in the other. This will be great!' However, it was a bet, and after all, who wants to lose a bet to their mother? Mark remembers, "By the grace of God, we thought, ok. Let's go to camp. Let's go mess with the Christians!" That was the idea. They planned to go, win the bet, be a complete disruption and irritate as many Christians as they could. God had other plans.

Upon arriving on Sunday night, they really believed they would be kicked out in a few days ... or hours. "We had a mindset," Mark recalls. "We always did everything to the extreme. It was our way of gaining attention. Whatever we did, we did all out. If you are going to be counter-cultural, do it the right way. Everything from our dress to our hair to our speech was screaming out 'look at us!' We fully expected to be ostracized within the first hour." When they walked into the registration area, the camp manager, Glenn, greeted them. Glenn Foster looked like an honest to goodness, Duke's of Hazard-watchin', American flag-wavin', pickup truck drivin', country music-listenin', corn-growin' good ole' boy. In case you're wondering, redneck Bible bangers and hip-hop dancers go together like peanut butter and ketchup. Mark just knew that a ticket home was inevitable, but God was already at work. Glenn, a man who I would eventually become friends with, was not what he seemed. Glenn was a sold out, compassionate, loving and devoted follower of Jesus. Service oozed from Glenn's pours. He never had a judgmental bone in his body. To their complete shock, Glenn made them feel right at home. Mark and Jeff were welcomed without even so much as a funny look. If anything, because of his complete acceptance of them, Mark and Jeff probably looked at Glenn with odd expression as if to say, "What in the heck is the matter with this guy?"

The surprises just kept coming. The first night was a bit quiet. No one really spoke to Mark or Jeff but no one was rude either. Despite their brazen attempts to be disruptive, make fun of others and flaunting their heathenism, everyone rolled with the punches and seemed accommodating. It didn't make sense. Mark thought, "Aren't Christians supposed to be judgmental and full of condemnation?" Not this group. Finally, a young man named Scott Browning introduced himself. Scott did something critical; he made an effort and made himself available. Scott sincerely tried to talk to them, he didn't judge and it was completely transparent to Mark and Jeff. This wasn't surface chitchat, this was genuine, "I care about you," type stuff. That night, based on Scott Browning's approach and Glenn Foster's acceptance, Mark and Jeff decided to really give the week an honest chance. As the rest of the week went by, more and more students approached them. As they interacted, they felt loved like never before. It's easy to feel loved when you are a performer. As dancers and rappers, Mark and Jeff gained affirmation and admiration for their talents but this was different. This was an unconditional love for no apparent reason. It humbled Mark. "Despite all the crazy things we had been into, we felt that, at the very least, we were on equal terms with everyone else."

By the end of the week, Mark and Jeff had given their lives to Christ. In one week, they had gone from, "Let's go mess with the Christians," to "Let's go become Christians." That quickly turned into, "Let's go tell everybody!" It seemed like a great and noble idea. It always does. Many people turn into evangelical sticks of dynamite the minute they are converted. Some people make a smooth and appealing transition and God uses their testimony in a mighty way. Others, frankly, shock and offend their lifelong friends (and complete strangers too) with their aggression and legalistic tactics. Instantly upon their conversion, Mark and Jeff went just as radical with their newfound faith as they had with their haircuts and use of baggy pants. Snapping, locking and popping (see the 80's guide to break dancing dictionary) changed into worshipping, studying and preaching. Unfortunately, even though they now served the Lord of love, you can take a boy out of the city, but you can't take the city out of the boy. Mark and

Jeff promptly returned to their old stomping grounds anxious to share the 'Good news.' However, as you might imagine, clubs full of drunken, hip thrusting, butt-wiggling youngsters aren't always receptive to the idea that they are, by their life-style, on the highway to hell. It always dampens the spirit to imagine oneself fall-ing into an infinite lake of blazing combustion. It didn't take long for the new evangelists to find themselves in an occasional awkward state of affairs. Mark recalls, "One time we actually beat a guy down for making fun of our testimony." Fist fighting for Jesus may make for an interesting documentary but usually falls somewhat ineffective in leading people to salvation. Nothing says Evangelism quite like a knuckle sandwich and a kick in the crotch. While some crowds were understandably unreceptive, the people that heard them at churches, youth gath-erings, high schools and conventions were wound up, inspired and energized by these young, dynamic revolutionaries and their 'in-your-face' challenges.

Mark and Jeff were just being who God made them to be. They preached hard, studied fanatically, wrote, and recorded hip-hop music to express their zeal. The hook to one original song was, "God is God, that's how it is brother, like it or not." However, as you can imagine, the 'in-your-face' approach didn't sit well with some church leadership and was even more offensive to most traditionalists. Mark says, "If that's your heart and you sincerely say to God, 'Here I am, use me,' you'd better fasten your seat belt." Being different usually draws criticism. It was as true in Jesus' time as it is today. Jesus was different. So different, in fact, that a nation wanted his blood. His disciples were different. Peter was just a blue-collar, redneck fisherman who would've been completely excited about Mark and Jeff's "Fist fights for Jesus" program. John, the "beloved," was a zealot as was James and Judas. The Zealots were about as radical as they came in that day. Then there was Paul, a man of high culture who, after his conversion, turned counter cultural. When you swim upstream in the church, people will talk about you. You will offend and you may even be disliked or even hated. Nevertheless, if nobody is talking about you, for the good or the different, maybe you're not doing much. Nearly every one of our biblical heroes had a fault or made mistakes that are obvious in scripture. Mark and Jeff were no different. Mark recently reflected on his first days as an excited young evangelist, "We may have done cer-tain things differently but one thing is certain: We were going do some-thing—screw up or do well—we were going do something because we were chasing after God."

Mark is one of my closest friends today. As an only child, he is the closest thing to a brother I have ever known. I performed his wedding ceremony, I consider him family, and I respect Mark. He has always spoken the truth, even when the truth wasn't the most popular thing to say. I remember him preaching a sermon in an old, legalistic, traditional church once. Mark never held back, he didn't know how to preach 'nice.' Mark boldly preached against things like legalism and traditions. I remember him saying, "I'm going to step on a lot of toes tonight, but I believe that God can heal your feet." Mark's legacy will not be that of a diplomat or a peacemaker, but make no mistake; the thousands of young people who first met Jesus through his sermons will remember him. Mark Lukhard is real. Mark Lukhard is different. Real different.

As you read this book, I want to encourage you to be who you are. Be motivated to serve him with what he has given you—just as you are. Joseph Campbell said, "The privilege of a lifetime is being who you are." That is so true. God made you uniquely for a reason. He wants to speak through you to specific people for specific reasons. We should be more concerned about being real than saying and doing "all the right things." Study his Word, know it and share it. People may not always agree with you, but if you are being real, they will respect you. Dr. Seuss, a man who embraced his distinctiveness, said, "Be who you are, and say what you feel, because those who mind don't matter, and those who matter don't mind." God created you, exclusively, to be who you are and to say what he would have you say (give your testimony). He is the one who matters most. He can use your testimony in a mighty way. You are special. I implore you; please, please, please … stay that way.

Authenticity is an incredible and beautiful thing. Why we try to squelch it is a mystery to me. If you were an inch shorter, you wouldn't be you. If your eyes were green instead of blue, you wouldn't be you. If you didn't have your great sense of humor, you wouldn't be you. If you hadn't failed the first time you tried something challenging (and the second time), you wouldn't be you. If you hadn't succeeded numerous tries later, you wouldn't be you. If you hadn't experienced that heartache you suffered a while back, you wouldn't be you. If you hadn't had children, you wouldn't be you. If you hadn't gone through that divorce, you wouldn't be you. If you hadn't heard those words of encouragement years ago, you wouldn't be you. If you hadn't lost that loved one, you wouldn't be you.

If God made you anyone else, you wouldn't be you. Why we try to be someone other than who we are, I don't know. Why we try to deny our failures, I don't know. Why we try to do what everyone else does, I don't know. Why we are scared to be different, I don't know. At the core of this enigma is the old saying, "The biggest obstacle anyone has to overcome is their own attitude about themselves."

You are you for a reason. You are special and you are wanted. I've often heard preachers say, "God doesn't NEED you." I understand why they are saying that, and I recognize that God can do whatever he has to do in order to accomplish his tasks with or without us. However, I think our willingness to serve and allow him to work through us makes his job a lot easier. Coldly saying God doesn't need us, without explanation, diminishes his love for individuals I think. In Luke 15, Jesus tells the Pharisees just how important we are (even "sinners") to God. *"Suppose one of you has a hundred sheep and loses one of them. Does he not leave the ninety-nine in the open country and go after the lost sheep until he finds it? And when he finds it, he joyfully puts it on his shoulders and goes home. Then he calls his friends and neighbors together and says, 'Rejoice with me; I have found my lost sheep.' I tell you that in the same way there will be more rejoicing in heaven over one sinner who repents than over ninety-nine righteous persons who do not need to repent."* Perhaps God doesn't need us, but make no mistake; He loves you more than you can imagine. He is passionate about you and your abilities and he is fervent about your role in his work. You are the apple of his eye!

Think about the story of creation in Genesis. God created all things, named them, gave them different qualities, sounds, colors and abilities. In the beginning, God came up with, and made, the heavens and the earth. He thought up and made light, dark, the waters, the heavens, the dry lands, vegetation, fruit trees, the sun, the moon, swarms of creatures in the seas, birds, cattle, creeping things, and beasts of the field. God thought up and made laws which rule the things that were made, how they move, slow down, and stop; how things can ignite and be transformed into other things; forces that pull apart and attract. God continued to think and to make up even more laws, among them, laws that control sounds and the ways they differ; the ways they transmit. God made every diverse sound; whistling sounds, growls, screeches, grunts, roars, and yaps and he liked what he heard. He created colors and painted the earth and all of creation with a palette of hues and tints too many to consider. He mixed and splattered, stroked and brushed with an artistic mastery beyond compare and he liked what he saw.

Then, on the sixth day, God went one step further. Genesis 1:26–31 says, *"Then God said, "Let us make man in our image, in our likeness, and let them rule over the fish of the sea and the birds of the air, over the livestock, over all the earth, and over all the creatures that move along the ground." So God created man in his own image, in the image of God he created him; male and female he created them. God blessed them and said to them, "Be fruitful and increase in number; fill the earth and subdue it. Rule over the fish of the sea and the birds of the air and over every living creature that moves on the ground." Then God said, "I give you every seed-bearing plant on the face of the whole earth and every tree that has fruit with seed in it. They will be yours for food. And to all the beasts of the earth and all the birds of the air and all the creatures that move on the ground—everything that has the breath of life in it—I give every green plant for food." And it was so. God saw all that he had made, and it was very good."*

Notice the last sentence. God creates all week long and says, "It is good," at the end of each day. However, at the end of day six, God had given life to creation in his own likeness (You and me) and he says, "It is VERY good." Above the beauty of the canyons, the brilliance of the sun and the depths of all the galaxies of the universe, you are the pride of his creation. Truly, he saved his best for last. You! You are like a dishwasher. It's true. God designed us in a way that is comparable to a dishwasher. Now, let me explain that statement. When I was 28 years old, I found myself in Charlotte, North Carolina working in the youth ministry trenches just before I entered into associate ministry in Florida. A month or so before moving I went looking at apartments. I had rented places before, but as soon as I walked inside the Catawba apartments in Belmont, I was sold. The lady showing me the various layouts and options took me inside a two bedroom, third floor apartment with a great view. The cool part was when she showed me the kitchen. "This is your dishwasher," she said. "Dishwasher?" I asked having never had one in my previous rentals or at home while growing up. Actually, growing up at home, I was the dishwasher. "You've never had one?" she asked. I told her that I had not. "You're going to love this then." She went on to show me how it worked. She opened the door and pointed to a little box, "You just squirt your soap in here, shut the door and that's it." "That's it?" I asked, "Does it work good?" She smiled and shook her head, "When you pull those dishes out, it'll be like that old commercial, you'll be able to see your own reflection on your plates." "I'll take the apartment," I said before we even talked about price.

"28-year old bachelor" usually translates into "Idiot" around the kitchen. I certainly had no idea what I was doing. I went to Wal-Mart and bought soap (just like the lady said) to put into my dishwasher. In hindsight, I probably should have bought dishwashing detergent. What I bought was more like hand soap or something of that nature. I came home, put my dishes in, squirted some soap into the box, shut the door and went into my living room to watch TV and snack a bit. After about ten minutes, out of the corner of my eye, I saw a large white object seeping out of my kitchen. I ran in to find a giant "sud monster" rapidly approaching and gaining strength. I was quickly reminded of a movie from my childhood ... "The Blob." Armed only with a dishrag and a Slim Jim, I attacked "The Blob" face first. I somehow managed to find the cancel button and the creature of suds was defeated. It suddenly occurred to me that I had put the wrong stuff in the soapbox.

Most people would have just gone back to the store and bought the right stuff. Not me. My kitchen was already a mess, so I thought, "I wonder what would happen if I put mustard in there?" I sprung into action, nearly giddy over the vision of a yellow giant beast crawling from the bowels of my dishwasher. I anticipated shouting, "It's alive! It's alive!" just like Dr. Frankenstein had done in another film from some point in time during my teen years. However, much to my dismay, fifteen minutes after the operation, there were no signs of life. I crept, petrified, towards the dishwasher with one arm extended in the direction of the growling machine. Against my better judgment, I opened the door in mid-cycle. The rumbling ceased and steamed emerged. Then it hit me; the nastiest stench imaginable. Dr. Frankenstein's fiendish creation sown of dead humans couldn't have smelled this bad. I pulled one plate from the depths of ground zero. Covered in a slimy, golden film, the plate completely reeked. It was disgusting.

After I tried the same experiment with mayonnaise and grape jelly, I returned to Wal-Mart to purchase some Palmolive. Suffice to say, it worked wonderfully. The lady who originally introduced me to the dishwasher was right too. I pulled out a plate, held it up to the light and I really could see myself. God has made you the same way. He created in you a place in your heart (a box or compartment) designed as his abode. This void, as I've often heard it called, is a place that God alone belongs. Unfortunately, we often fill it with all the wrong things. We use everything from money to earthly relationships to hobbies to, in some cases, things that are incredibly detrimental. Some use foreign religions, alcohol, sexual indulgences, food binges and even drugs. When God is not where he belongs in our lives, we often chase after everything else in hopes of filling the void. However, when we place anything else but God in the center of our being, it's just like putting mustard into the dishwasher. The mess is unbelievable—but avoidable.

God is crazy about you! In Colossians, Paul calls us *"God's chosen people."* The book of Romans tells us that as God's children we are *"Heirs of God and co-heirs with Christ."* I Peter says, that you are a part of a *"called generation."* Ephesians says that we are his *"dearly loved children."* Moreover, beyond words, God esteemed us with such great love and compassion, that while we were still sinners, he sent his only child to this earth to die for us. If that doesn't make you special, I don't know what does. God desires to fill the void in your life and be the center. He loves you no matter what you did yesterday, last week or last year. No matter what you did twenty years ago, no matter what you did earlier today, he will love you for the rest of your days. He's crazy about you.

Fathers love to see themselves in their children. One of the happiest moments of my life was the day I became a father. There were so many great things about the entire experience. We were blessed to deliver at the Williamson Medical Center in Franklin, Tennessee. I cannot imagine a hospital providing any better care anywhere. They were awesome in every way. At 1:45 a.m., they told us we would be "having a baby sometime today." Less than four hours later, at 5:40 Brooke was born. The moment that our doctor delivered her and picked her up, Laura said, "Look, your chin!" I noticed that Brooke had a small dimple on her chin, just like mine. She had my chin. I was in love the moment I saw her. Now that I have three lovely little girls, nothing makes my day happier than when a stranger sees us together and says, "Those girls are adorable. They are simply beautiful. They look just like you." Personally, I think that is a bit of an oxymoron. You know, the words beautiful and adorable have rarely been associated with me. Nonetheless, I love it when people tell me that. I'm a proud dad.

So is God. Your heavenly Father feels that same way about you. The moment he created you, he was in love. He proved that love for you two thousand years ago when he placed his only child on this earth with an objective that would end in brutality and slaughter. When God created you, he decided that you were so special that he would sacrifice his only child in order to save you. You are designed like a dishwasher. God wants to be in the soapbox and he wants to permeate every corner and crevasse of your life. As cheesy as this may sound, his desire is to hold you up to the light and see his reflection. He desires to see himself in you.

He loves it. He wants to use you, the real you, the way he made you. You don't have to be perfect, great or even any better than you are right now. That's irrelevant. How perfect was David? Being an adulterer and a murderer aren't positive traits for any servant of God. How great was Paul—namely when he was Saul of Tarsus? I, personally, would question God's willingness to use me if I were killing his followers, impaling them and lighting them on fire ... but that's just me. Despite their imperfections, God worked through them to do his will in an awesome way. He will use you too. He is your Father and he believed you were worth the death of his own son even with your sins. If that doesn't make you special, I'm not sure what does.

Something else that makes you special is the people that you know. God not only has you where he wants you and needs you, but he has also placed people around you who would benefit incredibly from your service and testimony. He has positioned many people in your life who need someone just like you to talk to, share with and truly understand and empathize. Every time someone calls you and asks for help, you have a chance to impact that person. You will either affect them in a positive way and allow God to minister to them through you or you'll refuse and adversely affect them eternally. You have, therefore, an awesome responsibility. You can reach people that I will never meet, you can reach people that your minister may never know and you can reach people that your church may not. Your circle of people, places and things are unique. Your gifts, talents and personality are too. That said, that exceptional ability and persona that you possess is useless if you don't share with those around you. David Viscott perfectly broadcast this truth when he said, "The purpose of life is to discover your gift; the meaning of life is to give it away."

Years ago I met a man at a convention in Michigan who told me, "The two most important traits you can have is a heart for the people in your life and an unabashed love for Christ." In short, love people and love Jesus. The first thing I thought of when he said that, of course, was Matthew 22: 34–40. *" Hearing that Jesus had silenced the Sadducees, the Pharisees got together. One of them, an expert in the law, tested him with this question: "Teacher, which is the greatest commandment in the Law?" Jesus replied: "'Love the Lord your God with all your heart and with all your soul and with all your mind.' This is the first and greatest commandment. And the second is like it: 'Love your neighbor as yourself.' All the Law and the Prophets hang on these two commandments."* Love God with all your heart and love your neighbor. The longer I live the more I realize the importance this truth and the wisdom in it. I have watched people in my life burn bridges that later needed to be crossed. I've watched loved ones severe family ties, forever stunting wonderful memories irreversibly. I've seen friends hold grudges and carry bitterness towards others that love could have erased, making them godlier in the process. I'm not against righteous anger, but our anger is righteous. However, I am for forgiveness. Jesus once said; *"For in the same way you judge others, you will be judged, and with the measure you use, it will be measured to you. Why do you look at the speck of sawdust in your brother's eye and pay no attention to the plank in your own eye? How can you say to your brother, 'Let me take the speck out of your eye,' when all the time there is a plank in your own eye? You hypocrite, first take the plank out of your own eye, and then you will see clearly to remove the speck from your brother's eye."*

Jesus tells us plainly in Matthew 7 that the same measure of mercy and forgiveness that we show others will be used on us when God judges us. Life is too short to 'throw away' relationships. We don't have enough time on this earth to think we can get things straight eventually. We can't treat people any way we like. We are to practice forgiveness, model mercy and to love others. Past that, we are to love our neighbors as we love ourselves. Therein lies the problem. Many of us don't love ourselves enough to exercise this commandment to the full (and Jesus not only calls it a commandment, he calls it the greatest commandment). As much as God loves you, he loves others with equal affection and intensity. Being a servant requires us to remember that every time we see a strangers face. Every time someone acts like a jerk to us, we must remember that that jerk is special too. He made you special, especially you.

5

"GO BE JESUS"

A few years ago, I was on a road trip when I watched the movie "Pay It Forward," in my hotel room. To be honest, I don't remember much about the movie with the exception of the premise. The movie was about a boy who works on a school assignment that leads to social changes that spread from city-to-city. Assigned to come up with some idea that will improve mankind, the boy decides that if he can do three good deeds for someone and they, in turn, can "pay it forward" and so forth, unprecedented positive changes can occur. As the story progresses, the boy does his three deeds, time passes, and the boy believes that his experiment is a failure. Little does he know that a geometric avalanche of love and kindness cascades through the city and even beyond. Recently I spoke to an audience of 300 high school students and told them that if they were successful in pulling off the "Pay it Forward" idea, the first time they would reach nine people. That is not a staggering number. The second time, they would reach twenty-seven. That's good. By the third time, 81 people would have been touched in a special way. That's a Division I college football team. The forth time 243 people are changed, the fifth time 729, the eighth time nearly twenty thousand are effected, and by the fifteenth time, 43 million people would be reached in a positive way.

In contrast to such ethical rudders as "give them what they deserve," or even, "An eye for an eye", this movie's message was the opposite of what most moviegoers usually applaud. However, think about it; treating people with love regardless of whether they deserve it, isn't all that novel. Jesus instructed the twelve disciples, *"Freely you have received, freely give"* (in Matthew 10:8). Jesus wanted the twelve to pay forward the fruit of the blessings they had received. He expects the same from us. While we were still sinners, God poured out his love toward us through Christ. In Romans 5, Paul writes, *"At just the right time, when we were still powerless, Christ died for the ungodly. Very rarely will anyone die for a righteous man, though for a good man someone might possibly die. But God demonstrates His love for us in this: While we were still sinners, Christ died for us.*" God actively sought after our best interests even though we didn't deserve it. Now that Christ has transformed us, what are we supposed to do? Instead of repaying evil with evil, we are to pay forward his love and grace by overcoming evil with goodness. We are to love our enemies and to love even to those who desire to use and mistreat us. Best of all, unlike the premise in "Pay It Forward," we are not limited to three times!

There is no limit to what you can do for the cause of Christ. There is no scripture or commands that regulate the amount of times we are able to serve. God doesn't wish to curb your good deeds. He wants you to be you and to serve and bless many. You don't have to have a Master of Divinity degree to comfort the mourning. You don't have to have a Doctorate of Ministry degree to show mercy. You don't have to be on staff at the local church to evangelize your community for the cause of Christ. You just have to be available, willing and ready. God doesn't call the qualified; God qualifies the called.

What qualifications did Gideon have? In the sixth chapter of Judges we find out that before delivering the Midianites, he was hiding in a winepress under the assumption that God had abandoned him and his people. What qualifications did Jephthah have? In Judges, chapter 11, we learn that he was the son of a whore, his brothers rejected him, and he associated with the wrong kinds of people and made foolish vows. What qualifications did David have? He was physically tiny, and a musician who was 'prudent in speech.' That sounds more like the resume of a pixie than that of a giant slayer. What qualifications did Peter have? Peter was a hotheaded fisherman who denied Jesus to his face in his most crucial hour. What qualifications did Paul have? Paul was a killer of Christians and persecutor of the church. Most of us don't have that type of red flag on our resumes. God has called you to do work for him, to use your talents for him and God wants you to serve him. You are qualified.

I want to challenge you: Find and take advantage of every opportunity you can, every day, to just, simply, serve. Ask yourself, "Is there someone that I can help?" "Is there a gift that I'm not using?" "Has God blessed me with some talent that I have buried?" "Have numerous people commented on one of my strengths?" "Might that be a message from God about his will for my life?" Ask yourself questions like, "Do my neighbors know me as someone who they can turn to for help?" "Do people at work come to me for advice or help?" "Do they know that I am a Christian?" "Does anyone?" Think about it. How can you make a difference in the lives of others? How will your story read when your life is over? What will your legacy be? More importantly, what will Jesus see in you? What will God think of your life and what you have done with it?"

I thought that this would be a great spot for a story about some legendary servant for the cause of Christ. Maybe a story about a selfless crusader known throughout the world for his or her faithful service would be moving. Perhaps a reminder from scripture about how one of God's many Biblical heroes would serve as a motivator. Instead, I have decided to tell you three stories that you have never heard before about several people you have never heard of (and probably won't) doing things that the world may view as insignificant. The following stories involve servants who have no theological degrees or phenomenal talents and, yet, are making a huge difference in this world by serving God.

John Norman

One of my classmates in college was an anomalous person. John Norman was the very definition of mild-mannered. He wasn't a "Hey, look at me" kind of guy. In fact, John could have "blended in" in a one-on-one basketball game. To this day, I doubt I have ever met a more unassuming person. I first discovered that John wasn't your typical person, my sophomore year, one night when Mike Tyson was fighting on Pay-per-view. For a Bible College, there were an unnatural number of boxing fans in our dorm and on campus. The school librarian, Cheryl Lindsley, and her husband, Rich, were even into it. All of the guys in the dorm used to gather at the Lindsley house on fight nights. We'd all chip in a couple of bucks to pay for the fight and order some pizza. It was always a good time. On this particular night, however, the Lindsley's were going away for the weekend.

We asked around and tried to convince some of our professor's to host the event to no avail. Most of our professors (and especially their wives) were against the sport of boxing. One of my professors told us, "Boxing is barbaric, uncivilized and vicious!" To which one of my friends responded, "Yeah, so are you gonna watch?" My professor just frowned. Many staff members and professors told us that boxing was sinful. I see it as no more sinful than football. Many people assume that the goal of boxing is to inflict injury on another human being. This is easy to understand when watching professional boxing (especially in the Heavyweight division). Growing up, I watched amateur boxing with my father and have attended and worked corners of amateur boxing matches as an adult. A

point system generally determines the outcome in these matches. The fighters
wear huge gloves and, as a result, injuries or knockouts are less common in amateur bouts. Despite the many sermons and lectures against the 'Sweet Science,'
we all loved it.

After failing to find a place to watch the fight, John said, "My mom will let us
come watch it at their house." John's family lived about an hour north of campus
so we all loaded up in nine or ten vehicles and followed John towards Virginia
Beach. John was the first guy on campus to buy a Yugo. He bought it used and
wrecked from a salvage yard. We trailed John's little white toaster on wheels off
the highway into a less than wealthy area. We each silently began to respect John
more as we realized where he'd come from to attend Bible College. We knew
John was poor but this was shocking. As we drove a little further, it seemed to get
worse. We stopped at a red light and watched a group of about twenty guys in a
serious brawl. The next stop sign, a guy approached our vehicle in hopes of selling us some jewelry or some "Loco Lettuce." At another light, we watched the
police cuff a young man on the other side of the street in front of a liquor store. It
was right about then that the song, "In the Ghetto," started bouncing around in
my head.

Just as we had locked all of our doors and finished asking God to "deliver us," the
streets cleared and we began to see signs of comfort and hope on the horizon. At
first, there were convenience stores, some fast food joints and car dealerships.
Then we passed some very nice subdivisions. We began to breathe easier as we
watched as John's miniscule, imitation automobile turn left into an unbelievable
neighborhood. These houses looked more like castles than homes. One of the
guys in our car said, "He must be lost. Maybe he's asking for directions." John's
little car sputtered into the circular driveway of an unbelievable three-story man-
sion. He stepped out of his car and motioned us all to follow him. "No way," we
whispered simultaneously. "Where are you going?" one of our guys timidly half-
yelled. "Come on in, guys, it's alright."

"Now hold your stinking' horses" I thought to myself. "I have bought meals for
this guy at Taco Bell a couple times! He buys clothes at the Thrift store! He drives
a used Yugo for crying out loud!" I watched as the front door opened and his sister (who would also eventually attend Roanoke) and mom emerged, hugging him
and walking him in through the front door (or the Grande Façade in this case).
We followed in stunned silence. The front room was almost completely white. It

had all white furniture, tall bookshelves, marble floors and a white baby grand that was unbelievable. "Who plays piano John?" I asked. "No one," John said, insinuating that it was sort of like furniture. Just past the 'piano room' was something I had never seen in a house before: An elevator. Yes, that is not a misprint or a typo. An elevator. I half expected to see a guy standing inside there in a uniform with a stupid looking hat asking, "What floor sir?" However, to my relief, there was no bellhop. While a few of our guys walked out on the pier to see the Norman's boat (they lived on a small lake) the rest of us followed John into his parents entertainment room. This room wouldn't have been better if you had an hour shopping spree at Best Buy and a similar consuming binge at the Pottery Barn. It was astonishing.

The only thing more amazing to me was John. I knew John for a several years and would have never dreamed that he was from money. His father was a multimillionaire (as were several of his fathers siblings). Although I met his father that night, I don't remember a thing about him personally. What I do remember is finding out later that John refused to take any of his fathers money when he left for college—he wanted to make his own way. John took out student loans and waived on the prestigious educational institutions his family had access to, in order to pursue God's calling to ministry. What I do remember is his solemn and meek demeanor and the consistent joy I saw from John over the years. Every time someone needed something, John would pop up. Anytime there were opportunities to serve, John would be there. I saw in John the characteristics of Christ.
He was willing to leave wealth, to part with comfort and luxury, to become a servant. How many of us, honestly, would do the same? I took from John a unique respect that I will hold and recall until I die. I want to be more like John Norman. I want to be more like Jesus.

Tiffany Noesges and Crystal Orta

During my ten years of youth ministry, I tried to plan numerous service projects as well as the occasional missions trip. My kids did a lot of work over the years. Painting buildings, cleaning parking lots, raking leaves or shoveling snow for the elderly or shut in were the norm. However, the yards and buildings that we would work on as service projects were never the point. It wasn't really even as much for the recipients of the effort. These acts of kindness, both planned and random, were more about the life lessons and teachable moments that would occur during the deeds. Somewhat surprisingly, the results became predictable over the years. Sometimes the recipients, in their gratitude, would become emotional in the presence of our kids, thereby making our students and sponsors feel a sense of significance and self-worth. Other times, conquering a difficult challenge would require serious problem-solving or team work and our youth would experience trust, respect and unity on a completely profound level. Other times nothing happened more than an accomplished task, which was okay too. If you want to have a positive influence on your youth, laugh with them, hang out with them and play with them. If you truly want to teach them and establish unbreakable links with you and their peers, model service and serve with them. When they see you serve, they will see Jesus.

Once in a youth ministry, provided it is long enough, a student will teach you. I mean, they really teach you something. When it happens, it's rarely planned and never expected. It usually comes out of nowhere. When it happens, it's pure and unfeigned. It's real and it's unrehearsed. It's almost like the first time you saw your spouse smile at you (you remember, the first time) or like the first time your baby smiles. That's not to diminish those memorable and special occasions. It may even sound melodramatic or a bit cheesy to you. However, I will say this to you, when it happens, you will know it. This meteor flew past me once in my ten years of youth ministry. Once. Sure there were many flickers of light and faint glimmers, here and there, along the way and those were nice too, but on Thanksgiving Day 2001, my supernova occurred.

I was visiting one of our elderly folks in the hospital. Our senior minister was visiting family in Kentucky and he asked me to go by on Thanksgiving if I could: no problem. The old man and I visited for a while. He was a retired musician, a former band director and music teacher. He was full of stories. For the next two hours, he talked in detail about everything from music theory to World War I to Henry Ford. He also told me the most disturbing story ever about a bowel movement one of his co-workers delivered in the teachers lounge back in the 50's. It was incredible, but unfortunately for you, not something I feel compelled to share in this book. It would be unbelievably funny, but not at all fitting. As it became late afternoon, I told him that I needed to head home despite his riveting intestinal narratives. As I walked down the hall for the exits, Tiffany Noesges and Crystal Orta approached me. Tiffany and Crystal were two of my senior high students. They were carrying turkeys. "What are you guys doing here?" I asked. "We do this for the elderly every year," they said. "Visit the hospital?" I asked. "No.

We do that every week. But every year on Thanksgiving, we try to take turkeys to the ones that we know are alone."

Suddenly, I was in a beautiful field, green and yellow with daisies under a powder blue sky. John Denver waived at me and began to play his guitar. A choir of angels appeared on the hillside and I found myself skipping bare foot in a white gown. Surrounding me, dancing arm in arm in merriment, were Tiffany, Crystal, the thawed headless turkeys, an old fat guy in a leotard, the Dallas Cowboy Cheerleaders, my friend Kevin Barton and the Indian from the Village People. Bluebirds circled and smiles were on the faces of all as we sang the chorus of "All You Need Is Love" in gaiety. "HEY!"

I opened my eyes and I was back in the hospital facing Tiffany and Crystal again. "Hey! Are you alright?" Tiffany asked. As I returned from Neverland, I smiled, "I'm fine. I'm good. I'm okay." They looked at me as if to say, "Our youth minister is a dork." I looked at them thinking, "My job is not futile. I see God working in them. They 'get it'. I am looking at two angels. I am truly in God's presence here." They could have been anywhere. They could have been doing anything. They could have done whatever they wanted with their holiday but Tiffany and Crystal were putting strangers ahead of themselves. I felt such admiration for them (you know, the kind of admiration that a kid usually has for his dad or coach or youth leader). Until the day I die, I will look up to Tiffany Noesges and Crystal Orta.

The Gettig's

A few years ago, I led worship at Sylvan Hills Christian Camp, just north of the metropolis of Howard, Pennsylvania. I am not listing the actual city that the camp is actually in because I personally don't believe that a mountain with thousands of trees, millions of groundhogs and five old, rusted trailers necessitates a town name … it's just … you know … north of Howard. A good friend, Wes McElravy, was the dean of a small camp week at Sylvan Hills for about fifty junior high students. I arrived on Sunday night, got all of my sound equipment and my instruments set up and went to a staff meeting. Camp weeks like this one enlist volunteers and youth ministers from various churches in the area to supervise and work with the students. On this particular staff there were three remarkable people who would, over the course of the next few years, impact my life as well as many youth at the camp and their churches and communities as well.

The first guy I met was Scott Gettig. It was obvious to me in the first two minutes that Scott had a heart for kids. Aside from the fact that he has a van full of his own kids, his interaction with them was more natural than the majority of youth pastors that I know. It came as no surprise to learn that Scott was a schoolteacher. All week his love for youth and for Christ was palpable. His sense of humor and teaching were equally superb. In addition, despite his joking spirit, the students smiled at him with admiration. Students can spot an authentic adult a mile away and they can spot a fake from even further. Scott obviously understood two things. First, as a teacher giving his free weeks away to a group of adolescent pranksters in cabins without air conditioning in the middle of nowhere away from his family, he understood service. Moreover, he understood that goodness is caught more than it is taught. The Gettig story doesn't stop there. Scott had a sister on staff too.

Anita Tressler (formerly Anita Gettig) was the camp nurse. Anita was Scott's sister. Anita wasn't just a nurse at camp; nursing was her occupation. I didn't see her much the first couple of hours. She was, of course, behind the scenes organizing the kids' meds as they checked in and filling out forms and the like. However, by days end, I was taken back by her. Wes asked me to lead singing at the campfire at night that week. Leading singing also meant doing a closing song. The staff had handed me the lyrics and guitar tabs to their traditional camp song. They told me, "Anita will sing it if you just play. She's used to singing it unaccompanied." As the campfire ended, I found Anita and said, "I'll just listen tonight so that I can get a feel for it." The first note caught my ear and the second caught my heart. What in the world was a voice like that doing out in this murkiness? Obscurity is a place for singers like my dad, not Anita. "She belongs performing on a stage or in a studio," I thought. She has such a composed voice, really in control and enjoyable. Why wasn't she pursuing singing professionally? By weeks end, I realized that she was in her concert hall right where she was. God desires the heartfelt utilization of our gifts for the good of others. I can't imagine that he enjoys performers nearly as much as he does servants. Anita is a great singer and an accomplished nurse. She was also the mother of three including a son named Eric. Eric has special needs and I am convinced that Anita is on this earth to love and serve him. She loves her kids equally, but her face lights up in a special way when she talks about Eric. In a weeks time I saw her for who she was. Anita was a servant, using her gifts and knowledge where they belonged.

Finally, just before campfire, another Gettig showed up. Andy Gettig stands six foot three or four. He looks like he could line up with five offensive linemen and catch a short pass over the middle while avoiding a few linebackers. Instead of an NFL tight end, Andy works full-time as a fire fighter. Andy is the youngest brother. Andy is kind of like a 'baby big brother.' Later I found out that Andy was adopted, which connected personally with me. Andy spoke at campfire each night. Andy wasn't a Mark Lukhard by any stretch. He was confident and well spoken but not a dynamo like some of my old ministry mates. Yet, to my surprise, Andy had his own charisma. His messages were personal and very insightful. Watching him playing volleyball, directing games and sitting with the youth all week enabled everyone who encountered him to see him in a very different light than his physical traits would suggest. Most people don't view guys with Andy's looks (tall, dark and handsome) as servants. Most guys with Andy's brawn are more easily imagined delivering a knockout punch than a touching message. Throwing lumber or steel around would seem more picturesque for Andy than throwing his arm around a troubled, homely child. Most guys with Andy's skills would be anywhere else than an old Christian service camp in the middle of summer. Even though he was adopted, Andy was a Gettig too … and a servant. Imagine that.

A schoolteacher, a nurse and a fire fighter; Service isn't just a Sunday morning thing with the Gettig's. Serving is what they do with their lives, their vocations and their faith. The Gettig's have consistently written, called, emailed, opened their homes to me and visited me over the years. Somehow, the Gettig's always manage to slip a supportive card into my car at each convention, camp week and church event that I serve at with them. Anita even sent a card when my first daughter, Brooklyn, was born. I feel ministered to by simply knowing them.

What makes a servant serve? What makes some people put others first, while others never do? What makes one man consider others while another man puts his own desires first? A decision. It all comes down to an every day, every opportunity choice. That decision comes for those who seem to have an absolute resolve for service as much as it does for those of us who struggle with selflessness. People decide hundreds of times each day, to either serve or not. We all determine whether we will be givers or takers. By our own choices, each of us either says, "More of you and less of me," or "More for me and less for you, Jesus." Servants understand that they can be the 'hands and feet' of Christ when they see an unfulfilled need around them. Servants know that "a man can't just sit around."

If you want to do something special, you have to DO something. To quote J.W. Marriott, Jr., you have to "decide to decide."

On July 2, 1982, Larry Walters decided to do something. Larry was from San Pedro, California. Larry had always dreamed of flying but was unable to become a pilot in the United States Air Force due to his bad eyesight. Despite that minor setback, Walters was determined to fly. He realized that in order to make it happen, he would have to use any means necessary. He came up with an unorthodox plan when he was young. The flight idea included weather balloons, a lawn chair, a few sandwiches and a pellet gun. No matter how you add all of these items up, it equals a bad idea. Walters and his girlfriend, Carol Van Deusen, bought 45 four-foot weather balloons and helium tanks at California Toy Time Balloons. To avoid suspicion, they forged requisition from his employer, Film Fair Studios, saying the balloons were for a television commercial shoot. That is when the fun began.

Walters attached the balloons to his lawn chair, filled them with helium, donned a parachute and prepared for his first flight. He took one 'carry-on bag' of personals including a pellet gun, a CB radio, a few sandwiches, soft drinks and a camera. Unfortunately, when his friends cut the rope that tied his lawn chair to his jeep, Walters' lawn chair took off much quicker than anyone had anticipated. Larry figured that, given his weight and other estimates, he would rise 100 feet above the ground. He was a bit off. In a matter of minutes Larry and his lawn chair Were several thousand feet off the ground drifting over Long Beach; a slight miscalculation. Fearing a death plunge, Larry did not use his pellet gun. Instead, he continued flying and passed through the primary approach corridor of the Long Beach Airport. Planes flew past him, over him and under him. How scary would that be? Yet, at the same time, how funny would that be? Imagine being on a plane and looking out the window: "There are those buildings. There's the football stadium. Over there is that lake. Oh, and, there's a guy in a lawn chair!"

After a few hours in flight, Larry did get the nerve to shoot a few balloons. He actually descended somewhat slowly. His landing might have been perfect if not for the power lines. Larry's dangling cables tangled in some power cables, which caused a neighborhood blackout in Long Beach for about 20 minutes. Larry, however, did manage to climb down to the ground safely from his tied up "Air Chair." When reporters finally made it to Larry, they frantically asked questions.

After hearing Larry's story and dream to fly, one reporter asked, "Larry, why did you do it?" Larry replied, "A man can't just sit around."

We can't just sit around. Our salvation is not through works, but our legacy, as imitators of Christ, would be hollow without serving. Our example to those who know we are Christians is hypocrisy without selfless action. Active service is at the very heart of religion. James 1:27 says, *"Religion that God our Father accepts as pure and faultless is this: to look after orphans and widows in their distress and to keep oneself from being polluted by the world."* Many of us claim to be Christians and in our minds, we consider ourselves good people. However, without doing what Christ asks us to do and without being the people that he taught us to be, we are merely that, good people. I feel this culpability and remorse frequently. I know I don't do enough. I feel lazy. I know there are needs all around me. Perhaps you feel the same way.

Are we afraid to ask our minister or elders what we can do? Do we fear how much we will have to sacrifice if our minister asks us to do more than we bargained for? Have you ever said to yourself, "I'm not going to do that; It would take too long. It might cost me a few bucks. It's Sunday, and I'm not going to miss football. Help him? I don't even like him! I don't like doing that; maybe someone else will do it. What if I offer to help and they start asking me to do stuff all the time?" What we are really saying is, "I don't have that much time for Jesus. I don't have that much money for Jesus. Football is more important than Jesus is. I don't love Jesus that much. Maybe someone else will help Jesus. I don't want to be doing stuff for Jesus all the time."

We can't just sit around. In the Gospel of John, chapter 21, Jesus makes this point clear with Peter. Starting with verse 15, *"When they had finished eating, Jesus said to Simon Peter, 'Simon son of John, do you truly love me more than these?' 'Yes, Lord,' he said, 'you know that I love you.' Jesus said, 'Feed my lambs.' Again Jesus said, 'Simon son of John, do you truly love me?' He answered, 'Yes, Lord, you know that I love you.' Jesus said, 'Take care of my sheep.' The third time He said to him, 'Simon son of John, do you love me?' Peter was hurt because Jesus asked him the third time. 'Lord, you know all things; you know that I love you.' Jesus said, 'Feed my sheep.'"*

We have a responsibility as his followers to not 'just sit around.' Jesus' conversation with Peter must have been hurtful to Peter. I don't believe that Jesus' intention was to question their friendship. I do think that this was a challenge to Peter. When I read this story, I hear Jesus saying, "If you really do love me, go help my people. If you really love me, lend a hand to those who need it. If you really love me, assist the disadvantaged. Look after orphans and widows. Pay it forward. Do something. Serve! Go! Be!" Jesus tells Peter, *"Feed my sheep."* Notice that Jesus wasn't steering Peter towards inner achievement or self-improvement. Jesus wasn't focusing on Peter's talents; he was urging Peter towards the needs of others. Jesus was stressing the idea that service is not about our talents or ourselves as much as it is about how we can help others. This was the central theme of Jesus' life. Peter obviously 'got it.' While Jesus was on trial, Peter denied him three times, but after being face-to-face with the risen Savior, Peter learned to put Christ and others before himself (which was quite different for Peter). Peter was eventually crucified himself for preaching the Gospel. There are even writings that suggest that Peter requested to be crucified upside down with his legs broken, because he didn't feel worthy to die the same way Jesus did. As I studied this possible request by Peter, I learned that an upside down crucifixion would mean several things. First, you wouldn't die from suffocation or from bleeding to death. Instead of running down, the blood would often go to the head causing severe bloating and deformation of the face. Death would take an average of three times as long and would be far more excruciating than an upright crucifixion. In addition, I found accounts claiming Peter's wife was crucified beside him. I can't begin to imagine.

Anytime we begin to feel proud or good about our 'works' or service, we should try to remember what those that went before us went through for Jesus. Every time I find myself complaining I try to think about what real sacrifice used to mean. We are so sheltered, protected and safe. I am embarrassed when I think back on the times I grumbled and whined when I was in located ministry. It makes me queasy now when I listen to ministers vent about how rough they have it. "All of these elders meetings, and hospital visits are wearing me out!" "I'm so tired of all of the complaints from the old folks." "I feel like I'm at the church all the time!" It begins to sound like Charlie Brown's teacher to me. "Wa wa wa wa, wa wa, wa wa wa!" Ministry can be very demanding but, I mean, come on! I'm mortified that those sentences actually came out of my mouth. Yes, I'm the one who said all of those things. However, I can't take all of the blame alone.

At nearly every church I've ever spent any significant time in, I hear the following statement; "Ten percent of us do ninety percent of the work, while the other ninety percent only does ten." Sadly, that statement always seems to come from someone in charge. That is definitely a true statement in many churches but there are several problems with that statement. First, great leaders aren't whiners. Jesus wasn't a whiner. I really can't picture him saying things like, "Oh man, I don't want to be crucified! That would just be too much for me to endure. Don't make me carry that cross, it looks too heavy. Those nails are too sharp! I'm not doing that. Serve men? Hey listen, I'm the Son of God, I'm too good to be washing feet, touching lepers or hanging out with you commoners." How Christ-like are we when we complain? We need to save those haughty, narcissistic thoughts we hold in the depths of our core. You know the ones. If we're honest, most of us have those Pharisaical thoughts like, "Well, I've done this and I've done that." "I'm glad I'm not like those people." "I have gone to church all my life." "I lead small groups." "I can recite an awe-inspiring amount of scripture." "I've lead many souls to the Lord." "I have a degree in Theology!" Run that past John the Baptist and he'd say, "Is that all? Man, I lost my head for Jesus!" Do you think Stephen, Paul, or Peter will be impressed with all of your achievements? What would Jesus think? Most of us, at our center, could use a major dose of humility. Believe me, I know. I still struggle with the whole, "Less of me and more of you" mentality every day. Still.

Another problem with that "Ninety percent" statement is this: If ninety percent of your church is doing next to nothing, you are failing miserably in the areas of discipleship and evangelism. Aren't we, as his church, supposed to be modeling and teaching service? Leaders are accountable to a higher standard, and 10% wouldn't pass you on a test at Bozo the Clown University. Yet I hear church leaders broadcast their own ineptness with this ridiculous statement repeatedly. The next time I hear someone say that, I'd really like to say, "Well, Boo-freakin-Hoo." If your church isn't growing, don't point the finger at your minister. If there are no kids in your church, don't seek out a letter of resignation from your youth guy. If no one is coming to Christ at your church, don't slander your leaders. If nothing is happening for Jesus in your corner of the world, you blame yourself. It's your responsibility! The task is yours! Stop blaming everyone else. You are responsible.

The biggest problem is that we, his church, are not empowering servants. John Maxwell wrote in his book, *Developing the Leader within You*, "The more people you develop, the greater the extent of your dreams." Maxwell devotes an entire chapter to this idea. You may not have realized it, but as a Christian, you should have just as significant a contribution to your church as your minister. I'm not suggesting that you start writing a bunch of sermons to discharge on your unsuspecting colleagues at work or at school. Hosea Ballou said, "Preaching is of much avail, but practice is far more effective. A godly life is the strongest argument that you can offer to the skeptic." Each of us should have a ministry. Your Monday through Saturday should be the practice and example of your Sunday morning precepts. Albert Einstein once wrote, "Setting an example is not the main means of influencing others—it is the only means." We need to lead by our example. Others need to know these same truths. My dad told me at Myrtle Beach, "Sometimes people just need a little push." It is so true. You would be amazed at what a little bit of encouragement would do for some of that ninety percent who does very little. Think about what encouragement does for you. Ralph Waldo Emerson said, "Trust men and they will be true to you; treat them greatly and they will show themselves great." If we truly want others to prosper and do more than 'ten percent,' we have to encourage and empower them. This will lead them to action, service and unleashing their God given abilities. Johann Wolfgang von Goethe once said, "Treat people as if they were what they ought to be and you help them to become what they are capable of being."

My dock supervisor at the previously mentioned warehouse called Wetterau used to get riled up when he would hear people complaining. Many times, we would receive an interminable order late on our shift. We would all start protesting and carping, "This ain't right, man! We're supposed to be outta' here in a couple hours. This'll take an entire shift. This is a bunch of ..." (you get the picture). Our supervisor (who would have to help as well) would just erupt with frustration. "Just shut up and get busy!" he'd bark with tobacco juice soaring through his visible breath on those frigid pickup bays. So we did. Every one of us would bust his butt and nearly every time, we'd finish that order just about the time that first shift would arrive. Moreover, every single time, as we all clocked out, our supervisor would always be the last one off the floor. I doubt too many people noticed, but I did. He would always make sure that every man had done his part, put his things away and he'd clean up after everyone on the team after our shift ended. Sometimes it took him a while, but he had our backs and I respected that.

We need to have someone's back from time to time as well. When we put others first in the depths of our minds and in the center of our hearts, service becomes more of a natural reaction than a work. Next to God, my wife and girls are first in my life. Because my daughters are so prominent in my heart, cleaning up 'little

accidents,' changing nasty green diapers and mopping up lung butter after a pro-
jectile vomit in the back of my car have never bothered me. Don't get me wrong.
At times, the smell is like that of a rotting deer carcass. Nevertheless, I love them
more than I love myself. I would do anything for them. That said, since I am still
working on putting all others before myself, I almost certainly would not change
your pants if you should happen to have a ' little accident.' In Philippians 2, Paul
writes, *"If you have any encouragement from being united with Christ, if any comfort
from his love, if any fellowship with the Spirit, if any tenderness and compassion, then
make my joy complete by being like-minded, having the same love, being one in spirit
and purpose. Do nothing out of selfish ambition or vain conceit, but in humility consider others better than yourselves. Each of you should look not only to your own interests, but also to the interests of others."*

My charge to you is this; don't complain. Just shut up and get busy. Go be Jesus.
Just go be Jesus. While we cannot actually BE Jesus, we can be his ambassadors
and a picture of love, service and care for people who don't know what Jesus
really looks like. Many people are tired of simply hearing about Jesus, but a large
portion of those folks are open to seeing him. Even when Jesus was here on earth
it was that way. The sinners embraced him and the church rejected him. The
"lost" reached out to him, the "found" demanded his crucifixion. The pagans
wanted his forgiveness and the "Holy" wanted his death. That's because of what
Jesus showed to the sinners, the seekers and the unholy. The people around you
who aren't Christians need love before they need the Law. You, and your unique
abilities and personality, have a great opportunity to show them both. Go be
Jesus.

6

"THE 'IF AND WHATEVER' CONDITION"

I've been an Oakland A's fan since 1975. I'm an A's fan for the same reason that I'm a Miami Dolphins fan. I became interested pro sports in elementary school in the early 70's. Any sports fan knows how great the Dolphins were in those days. In 1972, they won 17 straight games including the Super Bowl to become the only team in NFL history to have a perfect record and they were champions again in 1973. The A's were even more successful on the baseball diamond, winning the World Series three times in a row from 1972 through 1974. Just as I became a sports fan, all of my friends were saying, "The A's are the best," and "The Dolphins are the best." I believed them; just in time for the championships to end. I remained loyal to my two far away franchises from first grade through high school in an Oriole and Redskin loving Hagerstown, Maryland. This was especially hard in high school. The Orioles became champions and the A's became the laughing stock of baseball. To make matters worse, those stinking Redskins manhandled my beloved Dolphins in Super Bowl XVII, 27–17, my sophomore year. I rode the bus to school the following morning amidst a jovial cult of Skins fans who pointed and laughed at me as though my pants had fallen off as I hopped on the bus. Seriously, riding to school naked would have been far less humiliating for me.

Finally, in 1988, the A's returned to the World Series and I was ready to taste the glory of a World Championship for the very first time. Unfortunately, Kirk Gibson and the Los Angeles Dodgers got in the way and ultimately ruined my fun. Thank goodness, I was a freshman in college by then so there would be no bus ride through Redskin hell this time. There weren't a ton of Dodger fans on the coast of North Carolina. The night after the last game is what I will never forget. I sat in the student center at Harold C. Turner (my dorm at my college) and

84

watched Johnny Carson welcome the Most Valuable Player from the Dodgers, a young pitcher named Orel Hershiser to the stage. I was ready to throw a tomato at the TV. Disgusted with the whole situation, I wasn't about to give this guy a chance at all. He was one of the jerks that prevented me, and the Oakland A's, from baseball championship glory! As Orel walked out, the Los Angeles studio audience, most of whom were Dodger fanatics, went bananas. After the lengthy ovation, Johnny asked a bunch of questions about the Dodgers huge upset victory. It was sickening for me. It was bad enough that I had suffered for a week through the Series, painfully awaiting a remedy that would never come; now I had to sit in agony watching this incurable disease mock me on national television. I was just about to leave when something happened. "I read something in the paper that when you get a little distressed and you want a little control ... you sing to yourself," Johnny said. "You sing some hymns?" The entire student center at our small Bible College got a bit quieter in anticipation of Hershiser's response.

The young pitcher stood, without explanation, and sang the following song in front of millions of late night viewers:

"Praise God from whom all blessings flow,
Praise Him, all creatures here below,
Praise Him above, ye heavenly hosts,
Praise Father, Son and Holy Ghost. Amen."

Instantly I forgot about the A's, lost my nausea and became wide-eyed as I leaned in to listen to this man talk about communicating with God. For a couple of minutes he wasn't a Los Angeles Dodger, a Most Valuable Player, or a dastardly scoundrel. He was another person like me, trying to be more like him. It surprised me that a man would talk and sing to God in the heart of an intense athletic competition. I mean, nothing says Doxology better than the pitchers mound at Dodger Stadium, you know? It rather brings to life Paul's words, *"pray without ceasing"* in 1 Thessalonians. Whenever I find myself thinking I need to pray, "I've just been too busy" is one of my first excuses. That said; if a baseball player can find time to go to God during the defining moment of his professional career, maybe I should find time. I would imagine God could understand a man postponing his prayer time in the middle of pitching the last game of the World Series. However, he probably would rather me let go of the last ten minutes of that "Sanford and Son" rerun and make time for him. I would imagine his insight is probably more valuable than Sports Center highlights on ESPN. Solitaire Yahtzee can wait, that late-night bowl of Apple Jacks can wait, and yes, my Nancy Drew DVD's can wait. We need to be more like Mary, who sat at Jesus' feet, than like Martha. Remember, Martha thought the kitchen work was more important than spending time with the savior of the universe. I'm like Martha more often than not. Yes, I have to admit (with a high degree of humiliation) Fred Sanford has taken precedence over the messiah on more than one occasion.

I've attended hundreds of church meetings over the years. I've attended staff meetings, elders meetings, ministers meetings, committee meetings, elders meetings about the committee meetings and those "meet because we have to meet twice a month" meetings. In those meetings, we talked about curtains, chicken, cement, computer programs, certain member's personal problems, vans, rap music, softball rosters and authentic German sauerkraut. Of course, curtain discussions must occur sometimes. I know that cement is an important topic when the church is laying ground on a new wing. I love sauerkraut, so to acknowledge its significance seems redundant. The sad truth is, I rarely remember much more than a brief opening and/or closing prayer during these meetings. What do you suppose God thinks every Sunday when millions of people end up in church but spend only a few brief moments in prayer? We have all of this important stuff to deal with but no time for prayer. How does that even begin to make any sense? The irony is that we, the church, are crippling ourselves. We are depriving ourselves, and all of those around us, of God's power. James 4:2 states, *"You do not have, because you do not ask."* Just imagine what would happen if prayer was the top priority of the church. We would see a big difference if prayer was even a top 10 priority with the church. You can do an honest evaluation of your priorities by examining how and on what you spend your time.

Honestly, I've watched three-hour football games my whole life, but I've never spent three hours in prayer. I've watched three different three-hour football games, back-to-back-to-back. With commercials and post game interviews, I've experienced ten to eleven consecutive hours of National Football League bliss. My whole family likes football and we'll probably always watch it. However, set a timer and you will be amazed at how long ten minutes can seem when you pray. That will give you some perspective. We all could most likely pray more than we do. Growing up I can remember our church having 24-hour prayer vigils when something 'important' came up. It only happened about once every five years or so, but when it did, it was a big deal. Looking back, I wonder if we could have done a little better. Instead of it being the event of the decade, maybe our church could have made this a regular part of their schedule like the Chicken Dinners and the Gospel concerts. You know, once every six months. Better yet, like Sunday school or at least like those "meet because we have to meet twice a month" meetings. In hindsight, maybe our church sang "Sweet Hour of Prayer" because "Sweet Four Minutes of Prayer Once Every Five Days" didn't fit the melody or rhyme scheme. What impact the church could make if most, if not all, of its members prayed regularly. What would happen if we, as individuals, really spent the time we should in prayer? One thing is certain; we would know him much better. James Stewart once said, "To the man who prays habitually (not only when he feels like it—but also when he does not feel like it) Christ is sure to make himself real."

I believe that time spent with Christ is one of the keys to discernment. The more we attempt to find God and understand his will; the clearer that plan will become most of the time. Jeremiah quotes God in his 29th chapter, "For I know the plans I have for you," declares the Lord, *"plans to prosper you and not to harm you, plans to give you hope and a future. Then you will call upon me and come and pray to me, and I will listen to you. You will seek me and find me when you seek me with all your heart."* God tells us he has plans for us, we just need to sit and listen. He has amazing opportunities for us if we make ourselves available and willing. However, if we never stop, sit and listen we'll never understand.

My oldest daughter, Brooklyn, and I went through this. When she was around 20 months old or so, she began really putting words together and started saying sentences. She became so expressive and spoke so passionately when broadcasting her ideas and desires. The only problem was she wasn't always very clear. One morning while Laura was in the shower, I decided to be Mr. Mom and make breakfast for everyone. I asked Brooklyn, "Brooke, would you like some waffles?" "Uh huh," she said, affirming my idea as a good one. I made what I saw as a delightful stack of buttery, spherical goodness. They were a beautiful shade of blonde with an even consistency and inviting aroma that would have made even Gandhi's mouth water. If but for a morning, I had created something so perfect, so faultless, so good. I was the Lord of Waffles. Wow. I placed one onto Brooklyn's plate and put it in front of her. She began to shovel it in to her mouth. She became quiet. As she consumed the waffle, I thought, 'She's speechless!' "How are they, honey?" I asked. "Awful," Brooke replied. I thought I had heard her wrong. "What baby?" I asked in sudden humility. "Awful!" she said. I was crushed. A toddler had condemned my floury, little expressions of love. I thought, 'I know somebody who will be eating Captain Crunch tomorrow.' Then I got down on one knee, looked her in the eyes, and said in defeat, "I'm sorry honey, don't you like my breakfast?" Then Brooke looked at me and said, "Uh huh, Good 'awfuls' daddy, thank you." It took a minute for me to stop and listen in humility for her message to become clear. When I did that, I enjoyed the conversation a little more. "Awfuls" were actually "waffles." In the months to come, I listened to my daughter call the Dallas Cowboys, the Dallas Moo Cows. She referred to M&M's as "Mun-a-Mee's." Moreover, my personal favorite, her most loved Christmas movie was "The Crotch Who Stole Christmas." The more I listened, the more I understood. I'm sure it has been that way for each of you who have been parents or ever spent significant time with any toddler. It is funny imagining Thurl Ravenscroft singing, "You're a foul one, Mr. Crotch!" Kids are the best. Sometimes, you just have to take the time to get down on your knees and listen.

The most important part of any ministry is prayer. The most important part of any job is prayer. The most important part of any task is prayer. The most important part of any decision is prayer. The most important part of any LIFE is prayer. The most important part of your relationship with Jesus is prayer. The most important part of your relationship with God is prayer. Prayer is the center-piece of your power as a believer and follower of Christ. Edwin Harvey once said, "A day without prayer is a day without blessing, and a life without prayer is a life without power." God is a giving God. He is actively working. He is doing things around us at all times and he is all-powerful. All we have to do is call on his name and his power is part of our arsenal. We only need to ask. In Luke 11, Jesus said, *"Here's what I'm saying: Ask and you'll get; Seek and you'll find; Knock and the door will open. Don't bargain with God. Be direct. Ask for what you need. This is not a cat-and-mouse, hide-and-seek game we're in."* We must communicate with him as much as humanly possible. Without communication, every relationship struggles.

What kind of a connection would you have with your best friend if you only talked three times a day for thirty seconds before a meal? What would he or she think if you only spoke to your significant other every now and then? How would you feel if he or she only acknowledged you in times of trouble? What kind of relationship would you have if you only spoke to your spouse whenever you felt like it? Some of you may be thinking, 'I only have to deal with my spouse every

once in a while? Sounds good!' If so, I can suggest numerous marriage enrich-
ment books and counseling services. A serious evaluation of that type of relationship would undoubtedly lead you to a much worse place in your life. I can't
imagine not having my wife in my life. We have had some epic arguments. We
have had our share of turbulent times. I mean we have really had our problems.
We disagree often. However, through all of those struggles, we have come to realize that communication is key to your relationship thriving. Every time we have
had difficulties, it has been due to poor communication. Every time.

Trials in life and love can produce deeper love and a stronger relationship in the
end. A friend of mine shared an illustration with me one day that made this visual
for me. In Ephesians 3, Paul writes to the church in Ephesus, *"For this reason I
kneel before the Father, from whom his whole family in heaven and on earth derives
its name. I pray that out of his glorious riches he may strengthen you with power
through his Spirit in your inner being, so that Christ may dwell in your hearts
through faith. And I pray that you, being rooted and established in love, may have
power, together with all the saints, to grasp how wide and long and high and deep is
the love of Christ, and to know this love that surpasses knowledge—that you may be
filled to the measure of all the fullness of God. Now to him who is able to do immeasurably more than all we ask or imagine, according to his power that is at work
within us, to him be glory in the church and in Christ Jesus throughout all generations, for ever and ever! Amen."* Paul says, I pray that you may be strengthened by
His Spirit, that you may be rooted and established in love and essentially full of
God.

If you are like me, you may not spend a ton of time studying trees. I know it may
be wrong, but I just don't. I was surprised to learn that many trees grow fastest in
dry season. A friend of mine shared with me that sunshine is actually a better
growth-booster than water for ancient forests. Studies have proven that some
trees in the Amazon rainforest grow fastest not in the wet season, but in the dry,
sunny part of the year. From satellite images, researchers found that many areas
of intact old-growth forest tend to 'green up' during the dry season, which lasts
from July through November. While most ecosystems thrive when water is plen-
tiful, a good diet of sunshine is the critical factor for the speedy growth of older
trees that have roots deep enough to find water. When the ground becomes dry,
the tree essentially digs a little deeper. It's roots dig into the soil until it finds
refreshment. The result is a deeply grounded and stronger tree than before.

This is not just merely a 'rainforest phenomenon.' It is true of our relationships and spiritual life as well.

Paul tells us in Ephesians that when we dig deeper we might have a better understanding of God. Understanding that Christ's love is wide, long, high, and deep, will strengthen our relationship with him. We must be willing to stop, get down on your knees, take the time to listen and be willing to dig when things get dry. It is in that prayer time and reading his word that we can come to the realization that his love is wide enough to hold all of mankind. The length of his love stretches from then until when and for eternity. It is alpha and omega. His love is high above the power of criticism and so deep that it is unfathomable and infinite. When we pray (and I don't mean when we say our cute, little, poetic graces) and get real in God's presence, the kind of powers we have access to, is beyond ourselves. Paul says, back in Romans chapter 8, *"The same spirit that raised Jesus is alive and active in our bodies."* In our relationship with Christ, we gain the miraculous, implausible, resurrecting power that he used to astonish the world. The cool part is, all we have to do is ask. Seek. Knock. Be still. Stop. There is a reason that God gave us one mouth and two ears. Communication with him is essential to effectively communicate with those all around us and to making a difference. Remember, he has a plan for you to prosper you and not harm you. D.L. Moody said, "Every great movement of God can be traced to a kneeling figure." Pray. For God's sake and ours, we must.

My favorite verse, since I was a kid, was always Matthew 21:22. I like what it says and I love the implication. The NIV says, *"If you believe, you will receive whatever you ask for in prayer."* I memorized that scripture in the King James as a 9-year old camper at Tri-State Christian Service Camp. Tri-State Camp is located in the gigantic municipality of Strasburg, Virginia. *"And all things, whatsoever ye shall ask in prayer, believing, ye shall receive."* Regardless of the translation, I love it. The Message puts it this way, *"Absolutely everything, ranging from small to large, as you make it a part of your believing prayer, gets included as you lay hold of God."* I think if I had heard this when I was five, I would have started praying for things like G.I. Joe with the Kung-Fu grip, a new bike and the ability to use "The Force." When you're 9 years old, this verse takes on a completely different meaning. I still had delusions of complete and total life blessings at my slightest beckon. Moreover, at 39, it means something more valuable than it did 29 years ago. All things that honor God help lead others to the good news and benefit souls are possible in my life in prayer with faith according to his will. Anything you ask for, you will receive if you ask for it with faith. That's a big "if." Many people can't get one past. Maybe my weakness (mentioned in chapter three) is a little more common than it would appear on the surface. My weakness was my faith. Deep down, in the base of your core, perhaps your weakness is your faith. Is there ever any degree of uncertainty when you pray? Do you ever pray and wonder what God is doing or thinking? Do you ever feel desperation when you ask something of God? I don't know you but I would imagine that if you were born here on earth as an imperfect human being, the answers to those questions are "yes," "yes" and "yes."

Faith may be the largest roadblock in an intimate bond with Christ and his people. For a time, it was true for Peter. It was true for Thomas and true for the twelve and they weren't the only ones. There is a great and sad commentary on faith found in Acts chapter 12. This story goes beyond the distrust of an individual; it shows the lack of faith of an entire church. Chapter 12 says, *"It was about this time that King Herod arrested some who belonged to the church, intending to persecute them. He had James, the brother of John, put to death with the sword. When he saw that this pleased the Jews, he proceeded to seize Peter also. This happened during the Feast of Unleavened Bread. After arresting him, he put him in prison, handing him over to be guarded by four squads of four soldiers each. Herod intended to bring him out for public trial after the Passover. So Peter was kept in prison, but the church was earnestly praying to God for him. The night before Herod was to bring him to trial, Peter was sleeping between two soldiers, bound with two chains, and sentries stood guard at the entrance. Suddenly an angel of the Lord appeared and a light shone in the cell. He struck Peter on the side and woke him up. "Quick, get up!" he said, and the chains fell off Peter's wrists. Then the angel said to him, "Put on your clothes and sandals." And Peter did so. "Wrap your cloak around you and follow me," the angel told him. Peter followed him out of the prison, but he had no idea that what the angel was doing was really happening; he thought he was seeing a vision. They passed the first and second guards and came to the iron-gate leading to the city. It opened for them by itself, and they went through it. When they had walked the length of one street, suddenly the angel left him. Then Peter came to himself and said, "Now I know without a doubt that the Lord sent his angel and rescued me from Herod's clutches and from everything the Jewish people were anticipating." When this had dawned on him, he went to the house of Mary the mother of John, also called Mark, where many people had gathered and were praying. Peter knocked at the outer entrance, and a servant girl named Rhoda came to answer the door. When she recognized Peter's voice, she was so overjoyed she ran back without opening it and exclaimed, "Peter is at the door!" "You're out of your mind," they told her. When she kept insisting that it was so, they said, "It must be his angel." But Peter kept on knocking, and when they opened the door and saw him, they were astonished."* Why do you think they were astonished? They were praying. They certainly had a valid concern. The object of their prayers was a devoted, God-loving disciple of Jesus himself. Yet, their response to this miracle was to tell Rhoda, "You're out of your mind!" Their weakness was their lack of faith. How much better are we? Do we trust God more than those early saints did?

An old mentor of mine once made a comment to me that really caught my attention. One night while talking on the phone, I told my friend Dan that God was so involved in my life that sometimes I couldn't determine if it was God every time or coincidence on some occasions. Dan told me that, based on his experience, he thought it was God. I told him that I was simply amazed at how frequently God seemed to show up in my life whenever I really spent time with him. I had been wrestling with this for many years. Do I really believe that God still moves that way? Do I think that he is that interested in my needs? Really? It's the right thing to say that we believe that God answers prayer. But, I mean, come on. Is that what we believe? Does he really still come up big for us? How much confidence do we really have in that? Then Dan said, "Listen man, acknowledging miracles is scary." I paused for a second, as this statement seemed to soak into my mind. We finished our conversation quickly because he was at his sons' football game. Over the next few weeks, I allowed that assertion to hang on my brain's wall and marinate in my soul.

What I am about to write about is extremely complex and I must acknowledge that many theologians have differing opinions on miracles. I respect the vast majority of those viewpoints. I don't know that I have an end all conviction on the specifics, I only know what my experiences have taught me and I am still learning everyday. Miracles happened all the time in the Bible. Do they still take place now? I've heard hundreds of opinions and scriptural slants on this topic as I have spoken at hundreds of churches of various denominational histories and doctrinal positions over the years. Some churches have told me flat out, "His Spirit worked that way then but not now." Saying God doesn't perform the unbelievable anymore is certainly a safer mindset. However, who has the right to put God into a frame or a container? People have actually told me, "God doesn't do that kind of thing now days. He just doesn't behave that way." Men make these statements as though they are a favorite verse. It reminds me of those big billboards you see on the highway that state a biblical principle in a sarcastic manner and they attach God's signature as though God said it. Church marquee artists and T-Shirt designers get in on that one too. How damaging is the witness of these corny, tasteless, acerbic taunts with God's name attached? I always react to those the same way … "What?" I'm pretty sure we should be careful about putting words in God's mouth. If we spent more time listening to people and less time bashing them or making them feel unloved, the unbeliever may know the love of Jesus instead of feeling humiliated by "His" words. Many theologians, just like the Pharisees, don't want anyone to be greater than they are, so they change God's words on their own. They operate on their own agenda and call it God's will. These guys claim to do God's will, while only doing their own will in Jesus' name. However, we read in Psalms 118:8, *"It is better to take refuge in the Lord than to trust in man."* Then I also hear skeptics and cynics make statements like, "God moves in mysterious ways." While that is certainly true sometimes, I believe we can clearly see God moving most of the time. However, my predicament remained for a long time. What do I believe that God can do? Is he more amazing than my comprehension or just a decent God? Does he still perform miracles and answer prayer or is he finished with us?

Jesus did say, *"If you believe, you will receive whatever you ask for in prayer."* That much is undisputed. That's not a billboard. That didn't come off a T-Shirt or a bumper sticker. This book contains many of my opinions. However, *"If you believe, you will receive whatever you ask for in prayer"*; those are Jesus' actual words. Jesus' claim suggests to me that I should be more open to God doing great things in my life. Jesus says that if I believe I will receive whatever I ask for in prayer. That, to me, implies the miraculous. Peter's church prayed for him, but they didn't believe it, even after God had moved! Acknowledging miracles is scary! It means that God can do even more than I allow him to. It requires us to let go and allow God to be in total control. It means we have to be open to him doing whatever his will deems right. It means embracing the "Less of me and more of you" mentality. It means that we may have to step back and be amazed. It means that we have to admit that this greatness is not of me. It means acknowledging that God is greater than we are. It means swallowing our pride. It means that you have to wake up each day excited in anticipation of what God will do next. It means surprise, wonder and astonishment. It means the extraordinary, the prodigious, the phenomenal and the spectacular. It means truly living and viewing God with a fresh sense of awe and respect. It means you may have to question your faith. It means that some of our traditional thinking may be selling

God short. After long consideration of my friend Dan's words, I imagine that for most people acknowledging miracles is, indeed, scary.

Something one of my professors taught me years ago, always helps me when weeding through the concept of miracles and God's response to our prayers. Another mentor of mine reminded me of this in a recent email. God is all-powerful; he is all knowing, and all good. I've met many sincerely good people of solid faith who are rocked when they prayed for something and got the "wrong" answer or no answer to their prayers. From seeing these kinds of situations, the issue can't be how much faith we have in every situation. Rather, it's the faith in God's ability and willingness to do what's in our best interest that we must consider. Sometimes we don't understand God's answers when they come because we don't have enough information to know why his answer is eternally best. My understanding of the prayer of faith, then, is this: it is the prayer that doesn't know God's purpose in a particular situation but still prays according to that purpose.

It's also worth noting that biblical miracles always connect to something beyond the miracle itself. This is particularly obvious in the New Testament. The miracles of Jesus and the Apostles always attach to some redemptive purpose. Usually it opens the door to an opportunity to present the Gospel. While sometimes sought out of self-interest, miracles happen with a different purpose. Therefore, if I am seeking God's purposes in a situation, I should be looking for something to do with eternity. This is the point where we start thinking about the fact that sick people are going to get sick again and eventually die, so what point did the prayer of healing serve, ultimately? Well, if it provided an opportunity for someone to come to Christ, it served an eternal purpose. Having said that, God doesn't have to make sense to *ME* to do what he wants to do.

Hebrews 11:1 says, *"Now faith is being sure of what we hope for and certain of what we do not see."* Peter said that he knew "without a doubt" that the Lord had sent angels to rescue him. By that time, Peter had gone so deep with Jesus that he had something deeper than faith; he had certainty. It's amazing to me that people are still thunderstruck every time God answers prayer. There is a difference between amazement and disbelief. To be amazed is to know God and have a healthy grasp on his power; to be in disbelief is a much different perspective. What do we expect when we pray? Why do we have prayer lists? Why do we have prayer groups? Why do we have things like prayer chains and prayer vigils? Corporate prayer requests deserve confident expectation. Earlier in Ephesians 3, Paul says in verse 12, *"In Him and through faith in Him we may approach God with freedom and confidence."* It should also serve as a tremendous witness when we see prayers answered whether it is a person having a successful surgery or someone in need finding a job. It's inspiring to look at a prayer list a few weeks after we pray—we can see where God has moved and answered. Obviously God doesn't answer our prayers exactly the way we want every time, but is it so shocking that he would actually move on our requests when we humbly ask? Without faithful prayer, we are powerless. With faithful prayer, we are equipped with a power beyond anything of this world. The second part of the afore mentioned passage in Ephesians 3 says, *"Now to Him who is able to do immeasurably more than all we ask or imagine, according to His power that is at work within us, to Him be glory in the church and in Christ Jesus throughout all generations, for ever and ever!"*

Faith is difficult for all of us on some level or another. However, faith becomes simpler once we have experienced that power at work within us. Just like Indiana Jones, sometimes we do have to step out into the darkness: a leap of faith. Sometimes we just have to step out. Sometimes we just need a little push when diving into untested waters. Like Martin Luther King said, "Take the first step in faith. You don't have to see the whole staircase, just take the first step." The more we exercise this muscle in our relationship with him, the stronger our trust becomes. Our roots dig in deeper and we become more firmly planted. In faith, we become more comfortable and acquainted with God and his will. In faith, uncertainty becomes less worrisome and the unknown becomes more comfortable. That is what trust in God is like. In 2 Corinthians 4, verse 18, Paul writes, *"So we fix our eyes not on what is seen, but on what is unseen. For what is seen is temporary, but what is unseen is eternal."* The Message translation puts it this way, *"There's far more here than meets the eye. The things we see now are here today, gone tomorrow. But the things we can't see now will last forever."* We must develop trust in our Father. That takes time and requires us to step out.

I'm sure Peter was remarkably happy to leap from the boat since he saw Jesus standing there on the waves. He probably didn't think about drowning or any other possible adversities. He focused on Christ and he trusted him. Most of the time, our fears and anxieties are a result of our own lack of vision: the things that are unseen. Proverbs 29:18 tells us, *"If people can't see what God is doing, they stumble all over themselves; But when they attend to what He reveals, they are most blessed."* Where there is no vision, there is no prosperity. Everything went south for Peter when he took his eyes off Jesus and focused on his own circumstances. I wonder how much more Peter trusted Jesus after Jesus lifted him out of the sea and into the boat. I also wonder if Jesus placed Peter back in the boat for a reason. He could have walked back to the shore and taught Peter along the way. He could have privately imparted a ton of knowledge to Peter. He could have further displayed the miracle that is walking on water. I wonder if he put Peter back in the boat as a way of building trust. When our kids fall off their bikes, we pick them up, tell them that we are there, let them know it's okay and, reluctantly, put them back on the bike and tell them to try again. Perhaps Jesus was telling Peter, "Don't be afraid, leap from the boat, focus and you can walk on water. I'm right here if you fall."

Faith inspires action. There is a story that I originally saw in a book by Leslie Flynn about a small Baptist church in New Jersey. In 1973 Pastor Ray Crawford and his flock of less than 300 people at Grace Baptist built a new sanctuary on a piece of land that had been willed to them by a church member. Ten days before the new church was to open, local inspectors informed Crawford that the parking lot wasn't big enough. The existing parking lot would have to double in size in order to meet codes. Unfortunately, the church had already used every inch of their land except the mountain (40,000 square yards anyway) that it sat against. Of course, the cost of doing this was far beyond what the church could afford. The next Sunday morning Pastor Crawford reminded the congregation of Christ's promise in Matthew 17, *"Because you're not yet taking God seriously,"* said Jesus. *"The simple truth is that if you had a mere kernel of faith, a poppy seed, say, you would tell this mountain, 'Move!' and it would move. There is nothing you wouldn't be able to tackle."* Then he added, "If you believe that, come on Wednesday night to pray with me that God will move this mountain in back of our church." Twenty-four people showed up. They prayed for 3 hours. As the meeting ended, Crawford told the two-dozen prayer warriors, "We will see you next Sunday as planned. I believe that God will be faithful." Talk about fortitude. Talk about guts. Talk about faith. Talk about a man who really knew Jesus. The next morning, the telephone company called. They were planning to erect a new building and needed some dirt to fill the marshy swamp they had on their property. Not only did the phone company take away 40,000 square feet of Grace's dirt, but they paid the church $25,400 and leveled enough ground for three parking lots and prepared them for paving. Years later, though Pastor Crawford has passed, the Church on the Mount has grown to over a thousand members. Pastor Crawford and a few members of his congregation had a trust in Jesus, his words and his Father. Like Peter, I'm sure that through their trust they know what walking on water feels like.

It is faith and trust that makes a man build a 450-foot boat made of cypress wood to withstand floodwaters from something that had never happened in the history of the world; rain. Only complete trust and full confidence can explain why three young men would walk willingly face-first into a man-melting furnace without hesitation. Trust is the only rationale or a skinny, young tenderfoot to drop his sheep and harp to jump in the ring with the undisputed, undefeated Heavyweight Champion of the Philistine Army. Faith is the sole cause for anyone to believe that the best way to knock down a great and indestructible fortress is to walk around it for six days and then play a trumpet until it simply gives way. How does the weakest guy in the weakest tribe of Israel defeat the Midianites with a couple hundred of his friends? How could an innocent and sinless man subject himself to wrongful persecution and a brutal crucifixion when he could have summoned every warrior from the heavens to lead him to victory? Faith. Trust. Obedience. Communication. And love.

When you are truly walking with Christ and ready to do so in sincere faith, he may very well call you to something that is completely out of your comfort zone. It may not make any sense to you. You may pray for another way as Jesus did in the garden the night before his death. It may be scary, it may be dangerous, it may be impossible to your mind and it may even seem extremely risky. God isn't always safe, but make no mistake, he is good. I often used to say to God, "Show me what can happen and I'll believe." That is what I needed. Sometimes I still need that safety net. However, God tells us "Believe and I will show you what can happen." Instead of us telling God, "Show me your will and I will be obedient," God tells us, "Obey and I will show you my will." When that sort of conversation takes place and we witness God working all around us, our faith becomes stronger and obedience leads us to accomplishing missions far beyond our own capability. We must pray and believe.

When I was a very young kid, I watched many rerun black and white television shows. "I Love Lucy," "Leave It to Beaver," "Dennis the Menace." I liked "My Favorite Martian," "The Andy Griffith Show" and loved "Mr. Ed." Another one of my favorites was a show called, "Father Knows Best." The show aired in the 1950's. In contrast to most other family comedies of the period, in which one of the other parents was a blundering idiot, both Jim and his wife Margaret were shown to be thoughtful, responsible adults. When a family crisis arose, Jim would constantly provide a warm smile and some sensible advice. Even as a child, the tales of the Anderson family kept my attention as well as any other show. Over the years, I have often heard that phrase, "Father Knows Best." As a father myself, I hope at the very least I can offer warmth and good advice to my kids. Sometimes I think I would give them the world if I could. That is a natural feeling as a parent and as a dad. Nevertheless, we have all dealt with that type of kid at one time or another. You know the one; Mom and Dad gave them everything they wanted, every time they asked for it, everywhere they went. That kid that is always being dragged out of Target by his mother, kicking and screaming while he blows snot and tears in every direction. You know that kid. The one that is so spoiled, only a Catholic priest with a gallon of holy water and pea soup shield could handle him. You probably know where I am going with this.

We have to trust that our Father knows best. Having strong faith, a healthy prayer life and being obedient doesn't mean that God will give you everything you want. He is God. He is not a magical genie existing only to use his supernatural powers to meet your commands when you summon him. Many people act as though God is their spiritual vending machine. Just put in a quarter (or enough prayer, or service or a big enough tithe) and he will dispense sugary sweet pleasures and blessings. He is your Father. He wants good things for you and he always knows better than you do. I think we are too much like that spoiled, demon-possessed Target kid sometimes. We think that if God doesn't give us our way, he must not love us. We think that if we don't get what we want, maybe he isn't listening or, worse still, maybe he doesn't exist at all. We have our plans, schemes, and ideas about how life will become ideal and it all makes sense to us. We spend so much time meticulously planning our future. We know exactly how God should answer each prayer. However, God answers prayers in his time not ours. God answers our requests according to his will not ours. Proverbs 16:9 says, *"In his heart a man plans his course, but the Lord determines his steps."*

God knows what he is doing. As much as we may hate to accept it sometimes, he always knows more than we ever will. He knows what is best. In my teenaged years, I questioned my parents' intelligence. I thought that they didn't know anything. Of course, that was that period when I was convinced that I was the smartest guy on planet earth. I knew everything and while I didn't think my parents were completely stupid, they certainly didn't know half as much as I did. It is only now, twenty years later, that I realize just how foolish I was. Remembering that also reminds me that I still need wiser counsel than I am capable of by myself. Yes, you heard it right from the authors' book; I am really not very smart. Luckily, my Father is. God says in Isaiah 55:9, *"As the heavens are higher than the earth, so are my ways higher than your ways and my thoughts than your thoughts."* You see, God agrees that I am not that smart: especially compared to him. I mean if you compared my intelligence with that of ten goats, at least seven times out of ten, I would be in good shape. However, compared to God, I can't even begin to suppose. Somehow, Tony Almighty sounds even more ridiculous than that of the movie titles Bruce or Evan Almighty. I'm sure you can relate. Fortunately, when we do things his way, there is no need to wonder if we did the right thing. Proverbs 3:5–6 is one of those scriptures that I have always known but have not always really known. Each of us must experience it. *"Trust in the Lord and lean not on your own understanding, in all your ways acknowledge Him and He will make all your paths straight."*

My wife came across a poem that I thought was fitting. Some people come to know Jesus as their "Wonderful Counselor" because they have spent thousands of hours in sessions with him. Some people know Jesus as "Provider" because he has shown up repeatedly to meet their needs. Some people know Jesus as "Redeemer" and "Savior" because they have gone through more than you have and I would in three lifetimes only to be delivered by Jesus' blood and God's grace. I believe the words of this poem because I have prayed these prayers myself with similar results …

"I Asked"

Anonymous

I asked God for strength, that I might achieve.
I was made weak, that I might learn to humbly obey …

I asked for health, that I might do greater things.
I was given infirmity, that I might do better things …

I asked for riches, that I might be happy.
I was given poverty, that I might be wise …

I asked for power, that I might have the praise of men.

I was given weakness, that I might feel the need of God …

I asked for all things, that I might enjoy life.
I was given life, that I might enjoy all things …

I got nothing I asked for—but everything that I had hoped for.
Almost despite myself, my unspoken prayers were answered.

I am, among all, most richly blessed."

God desires your prosperity, your conversation and company. The more real and transparent I get when I am with him the more lucid and understandable he becomes to me. That means being specific and honest. Confession is a beautiful thing when you know that the one you are opening up to is accepting and affectionate. No matter what you do or have done, God warmly wishes you to know him and trust him as the Father he is: a caring Dad who loves his children. In Isaiah 41:13 God says, *"I am the Lord, your God, who takes hold of your right hand and says to you, Do not fear; I will help you."* I love taking walks with my daughters, late in the day when it's warm outside. Walking with them and holding their little hands is the best feeling in the world for me. The sunset is always pretty, the conversation is always good (and entertaining at their age) and the company is the best. They like going with me no matter where I am going and there isn't a place that I don't like taking them with me. I like taking them to the post office, the grocery store, to the park and on trips. What can I say? I'm a dad and I love my girls.

God enjoys walks with us. I'm sure he wishes we would take him everywhere. He's a dad who loves his kids. I urge you to spend time with him. Remember to get down on your knees and communicate. Nothing could be more valuable or powerful to your life. In Matthew 6:5–8, Jesus says, *"And when you come before God, don't turn that into a theatrical production either. All these people making a regular show out of their prayers, hoping for stardom! Do you think God sits in a box seat? Here's what I want you to do: Find a quiet, secluded place so you won't be tempted to role-play before God. Just be there as simply and honestly as you can manage. The focus will shift from you to God, and you will begin to sense His grace. The world is full of so-called prayer warriors who are prayer-ignorant. They're full of formulas and programs and advice, peddling techniques for getting what you want from God. Don't fall for that nonsense. This is your Father you are dealing with, and He knows better than you what you need."* Your father knows best. If we believe, we will receive whatever we ask of him. Whatever. In addition, he is able to produce results beyond our capabilities and understanding ... if we believe and pray.

7

"HIS WAY"

I still struggle with having the mind of a servant, I always have. My natural tendency is to think "Me" first. To say that I can be self-centered is like saying Michael Jordan is a good basketball player. It's just true. When I was ministering in Florida, this was brought to my attention in the midst of a frank discussion with the senior minister of our church. We had just left one of those elders meetings where I was merely an observer as the sacred cows made critical decisions and weren't interested in my opinions. After all, I was the young guy. It wasn't anything personal; it was what it was. They were good guys and I was an irresponsible kid. As we left the meeting, I was talking in a somewhat negative manner to our minister about the meetings in general. My tone was, at best, sarcastic. I've always been good at that. Our minister, Scott, listened for a while and didn't say much. His silence only made me go further. At some point, Scott broke his silence and said, "You know what your problem is?" What? My problem? I expected him to join in with me not combat my complaints. This really took me by surprise. I was sure that I didn't want to hear what he was about to say. It's funny how you can anticipate things like that, but I was very intrigued at the same time.

"My problem?" I said with a tremendous amount of arrogance. Then he said it. "You don't have a servants heart." Ouch … and can I just say Ouch again? I can't imagine what it feels like to be hit in the face with a sledgehammer, but I am positive that it could not feel worse than those six words did. I actually felt my eyes well up a bit and my heart felt like it went straight through my gut into the lower regions of my bowels. I felt like I was going to dry heave, if not vomit. Naturally, my defense kicked in. I immediately started thinking of instances when I thought he wasn't doing a good job. The truth is, if you start looking for problems with people, you can always find one or, at the very least, you can make one up. I was ready to start pointing the finger everywhere else other than at myself. "What?

102

What are you talking about?" I asked. That was the worst thing I could have asked. For the next ten minutes or so, Scott busted me on situation after situation when I had been selfish. Some of his statements were wrong and some of his information was born of misunderstanding. All the rest, like 90% of it, was true. I was staggered. My mouth went limp and my chin hit my shoes. As I stood there and listened, I was angry. Much like my conversation with Mr. Alligood, all those years ago in college, my ego was taking a direct hit and I didn't like it. I left without really getting into it with Scott. I just left him know that he was wrong and I was right (self-righteous more like it). As I drove home, however, reason once again took over. Maybe Scott cared. Maybe he saw potential in me too. As I look back on my relationship with Scott, despite one of the most hurtful allegations ever made to me about me, I know he wanted me to get closer to Christ. He wanted me to be more like Jesus. I was at the point where I needed what most of us need from time to time: a nice, warm piece of humble pie. I was lucky to have a friend who didn't mind serving me a slice. Nearly a decade later, I know one thing for sure; a servants' heart is at the core of making a difference in the lives of others. Even now, I'm sure Scott has no idea of the kind of impact his words have had on me. I also know, without a doubt that he cared about me. Now I can say it; He was right and I was wrong.

I wanted to be a difference maker; I was just going about it in ignorance. Moreover, it's not as if I've cornered the market on making a difference today. I still do many things out of ignorance. However, I have been lucky to be around some people whose ability to change others is evident. From what I have observed over the years, I don't really have a ten-step program to making a difference. I don't believe that affecting others is about the things we do as much as it is about who we are. It isn't about our religious performance. Regardless if you are saved or not, we are all sinners. We have to come to the end of our own goodness and realize that God is right and we are, very often, wrong. Becoming more Christ-like begins in our nucleus, in our foundation and in our hearts. How do we completely change our central parts in order to become servants through and through? It think a good place to start is with that "Less of me and more of you" approach. That was Jesus' purpose and that was his way. The people who really make a difference are the ones who use this mentality with God AND with his people. That's right. Try taking a "Less of me and more of my spouse" way of thinking. What kind of parents would we be if we truly adopted a "Less of me and more my kids" attitude? Imagine what would happen if we lived by these creeds; "Less of me and more of my next door neighbor." "Less of me and more of my boss." "Less of me and more of people who rub me the wrong way." "Less of me and more of my church." "Less of me and more of that guy at work who can't stand me." "Less of me and more of strangers." What would happen? You'd probably make an eternal difference in someone else's life. I think you'll find that those mindsets go well with the obvious: "Less of me and more of God." "Less of me and more of Jesus." Jesus endorses this frame of mind.

The Pharisees once asked Jesus how to be great. And even though they really were only trying to trap Jesus with his own words, Jesus gives them his answer, the essence of his way, in Matthew 22:34–40. *"Hearing that Jesus had silenced the Sadducees, the Pharisees got together. One of them, an expert in the law, tested him with this question: "Teacher, which is the greatest commandment in the Law?" Jesus replied: "'Love the Lord your God with all your heart and with all your soul and with all your mind.' This is the first and greatest commandment. And the second is like it: 'Love your neighbor as yourself.' All the Law and the Prophets hang on these two commandments. "* The path to greatness, according to Jesus, is to love God and love people. The Pharisees believed that greatness was their own religious performance. Jesus tells the Pharisees that the Ten Commandments (the Law) are great and to be honored but greater is the origin of those commands. Jesus essentially tells these church leaders, you can practice the rules with complete devotion until your dying day, but without love all you have is religion. Without heartfelt service, you just have a surface code of morals or a set of rules. The Pharisees were more like a scout troop than a church. Mother Teresa said, "God doesn't look at how much we do, but with how much love we do it." The Pharisees were doing all the right things for all the wrong reasons. Jesus suggests that they love God and his people (regardless if they are 'saints' or 'sinners') and that they serve God and his people accordingly.

The Pharisees faced two problems that we probably should consider when evaluating our own service. The Pharisees did adopt a "Less of me and more of you" mentality but in a discriminate manner. A Pharisee wouldn't have been caught dead with people outside of their religion, let alone help or serve them. They never understood why Jesus spent so much time with 'sinners.' In Luke chapter 6, Jesus once again, attempts to explain this concept to the Pharisees. Luke 6:27–37 says, *"To you who are ready for the truth, I say this: Love your enemies. Let them bring out the best in you, not the worst. When someone gives you a hard time, respond with the energies of prayer for that person. If someone slaps you in the face, stand there and take it. If someone grabs your shirt, gift-wrap your best coat and make a present of it. If someone takes unfair advantage of you, use the occasion to practice the servant life. No more tit-for-tat stuff. Live generously. Here is a simple rule of thumb for behavior: Ask yourself what you want people to do for you; then grab the initiative and do it for them! If you only love the lovable, do you expect a pat on the back? Run-of-the-mill sinners do that. If you only help those who help you, do you expect a medal? Garden-variety sinners do that. If you only give for what you hope to get out of it, do you think that's charity? The stingiest of pawnbrokers does that. I tell you, love your enemies. Help and give without expecting a return. You'll never—I promise—regret it. Live out this God-created identity the way our Father lives toward us, generously and graciously, even when we're at our worst. Our Father is kind; you be kind. Don't pick on people, jump on their failures, and criticize their faults—unless, of course, you want the same treatment. Don't condemn those who are down; that hardness can boomerang. Be easy on people; you'll find life a lot easier."*

The servant life: that was his way. The "Less of me and more of you" rule applies to God and all of his people. Modern day Pharisees still exist and they are among us. Haughty condemnation runs rampant in our churches. It sounds through bullhorns and lurks in the corners of our buildings. It echoes from our pulpits. It flows from the lips of our slickest gossipers. It's everywhere. However, selective service is not an option for us. Helping other Christians or people that we like doesn't make us wonderful people. That merely qualifies us as human beings. Besides that, who are we to judge, which people are and which people are not worthy of our help? Jesus makes it clear to us: love and serve people. Period. He doesn't tell us to love and serve people we approve of. How would that make any sense? Love those who you love? Love those who love you? Impressive. He never said we should only help those who are followers of God. In fact, Jesus practiced caring for reprobates and says plainly that we are to reach out to our rivals as we would for our very own selves.

The other problem for the Pharisees was the lack of love in their actions when they did act. We shouldn't serve simply for the rewards promised to us. I recently became aware of a situation that is all too common and extremely sad. In short, a very wealthy old man in Ohio recently passed away while he and his wife were at odds with their children. The conflict had raged for many years until the old couple and their children were no longer communicating. When the old man found out he had cancer, several friends of the family and other acquaintances (who we will refer to as "Sharks") began to surface everywhere to get involved in the lives of the elderly couple. Obviously, the idea of a healthy inheritance was particularly interesting to those who knew he was in conflict with his own family and that he would have to leave his wealth to someone. When sharks smell blood, they become very vicious and aggressive. When the old man died, his wife didn't even contact their children. The children learned of their fathers demise from friends and in the obituaries. I can't even imagine that. The sharks all gladly paid their respects and offered help to the lonely old widow. They now circle around her vessel in anticipation of her collapse so that they might become "loaded." It is, indeed, a heartbreaking situation. The sharks (who are more like snakes) only help her because of the potential for their own prosperity. They certainly don't love the old woman. Most of us, at some point, have done something nice for someone simply for the possibility of our own gain. I know I have.

Once I performed at a huge youth convention in Illinois. I helped emcee an event that featured Audio Adrenaline, DC Talk and NFL Hall-of-Fame legend Mike Singletary. While I was there merely for comic relief, the former Chicago Bears linebacker was to follow the two bands with his testimony. As I came off stage from doing my act and announcing DC Talk, Mr. Singletary approached me and said, "Good job man, my kids loved it!" I was in awe of him. If you've ever stood next to a professional athlete, it's not hard to be wowed: Especially the big guys. Mr. Singletary is a big guy. They didn't call him "Samurai Mike" for nothing. I said thank you and started to go on my way when the shark in me emerged. I grabbed one of my CD's and gave it to his daughter who had been impressed with my "Green Eggs and Ham" rap. I handed it to her and her face lit up. She said, "You mean I can have this for free?" Then, with my four rows of hundreds of teeth showing, I said, "Sure, just send me your dad's autograph sometime." Right then, as my words hit her young ears, I felt like a complete scumbag. What could have been a nice gesture turned into the exploitation of a child for my own gain. Yes, I was indeed a shark; a great white shark to be exact. I was only thinking of me. Suffice to say, I never received that autograph. I just hope she never told her dad.

Thinking of others was Jesus' way. In the book of Acts, Jesus' followers are not only called Christians, but they are also called followers of *"the Way"* (9:2 and 24:14). They didn't just have a pledge to verbalize or a specific set of views or beliefs. They lived in a different way. Unfortunately, Christians aren't known for their way anymore. Our political views, moral stances, intolerance of anything 'secular' and our hypocrisy define us. Ask anyone who is un-churched and you will find this to be fact. I doubt that being viewed as a prejudiced, hateful, narrow-minded fraud would be pleasing to Jesus. We must strive to live a life of love. Without that, people won't care if you have the entire Bible memorized. Sadly, as I think back on my Bible college days, a lot of us were more concerned about learning to be "right" than just serving and living a life of love. There are tons of classes and books on subjects like Revelation and Old Testament Prophecy and the theological beliefs of every cult and denomination; all of which are certainly worth our study. After all, Timothy says that we should study to show ourselves as ones approved by God (2 Tim. 2:15). I probably could have used more time studying those subjects. Guys who grew up in the church and knew the word were always tricking me. They would ask me things like, "How did Jonah get all of those animals on the ark?" Jonah. Then I would spend a couple days contemplating how Jonah got all the animals onto the ark. More critically, I wish there were more books about mercy and grace. I wish there were more courses dealing with loving those who don't know Jesus. I wish I had spent more time really pursuing Jesus and his way.

As I started writing this chapter, it occurred to me that Jesus referred to himself as the Way. In John 14:6, Jesus says, *"I am the way the truth and the life. No one comes to the Father except through me."* Walking, talking and really living his way is the ultimate apologetic and most effective discourse when attempting to lead people to him. If you want to be Jesus to the divorced single mom on your street, don't go to her door with your Bible ready to attack her. Offer to mow her lawn or change the oil in her car. I mean which approach gives you more credibility. Which approach would Jesus take? If you want to be Jesus in a pagan workplace, try doing your job as though you were working for Christ himself. Show up early, stay late and help your fellow employees. Or you could stand up on the lunch table in the break room and shout out something like, "You're going to hell, you godless generation! Turn or burn, you enemies of the Most High!" You know, whichever works best. The Way is all about serving, not slamming, sentencing or screaming. Greatness is about selflessness. Jesus is about altruism. The Way is about surrender, humility and service. Jesus was walking with the disciples in Mark 9:33, *"They came to Capernaum. When he was safe at home, he asked them, "What were you discussing on the road?" The silence was deafening—they had been arguing with one another over who among them was greatest. He sat down and summoned the Twelve. "So you want first place? Then take the last place. Be the servant of all."*

I'm not the only one who has struggled with these concepts. It goes against our nature to put everyone else ahead of ourselves. Greatness is being the CEO not the mailroom guy. We want to be the star Quarterback not the third string lineman. We want to be American Idols not a back row singer in the choir. While there is nothing wrong with achievement, awards and accolades, Jesus says that's not his business. Superstardom was never Jesus' way. Jesus came to serve and to inspire us to do the same. Matthew 20:20–28; *"It was about that time that the mother of the Zebedee brothers came with her two sons and knelt before Jesus with a request. "What do you want?" Jesus asked. She said, "Give your word that these two sons of mine will be awarded the highest places of honor in your kingdom, one at your right hand, one at your left hand." Jesus responded, "You have no idea what you're asking." And he said to James and John, "Are you capable of drinking the cup that I'm about to drink?" They said, "Sure, why not?" Jesus said, "Come to think of it, you are going to drink my cup. But as to awarding places of honor, that's not my business. My Father is taking care of that." When the ten others heard about this, they lost their tempers, thoroughly disgusted with the two brothers. So Jesus got them together to settle things down. He said, "You've observed how godless rulers throw their weight around, how quickly a little power goes to their heads. It's not going to be that way with you. Whoever wants to be great must become a servant. Whoever wants to be first among you must be your slave. That is what the Son of Man has done: He came to serve, not be served—and then to give away his life in exchange for the many who are held hostage."*

Jesus tells the disciples that power; awards and prestige are not the ingredients of greatness. Jesus says that greatness lies in the exact opposite. We have a tendency to want to be recognized. For some it is a self worth issue, for others it is a matter of abused power (like Jesus referred to in the last passage) and for more people than not, it is somewhat normal. We all want to be accepted. We like compliments. We enjoy admiration. We all like to hear that we're doing something good. There's nothing wrong with that in most cases. However, God's admiration belongs to those who serve others. Jesus essentially tells his friends not to worry about accolades or titles or trophies, he tells them to simply serve. Jesus tells them that giving your life for others is the epitome of greatness. *"Greater love has no man than this; that a man would lay down his life for a friend."* What would happen if we lived that way? What would happen if we took that principle a step further? Are we even capable of doing so? We are, and I have proof.

Felipe and Donna

Felipe Garza, Jr. started dating Donna Ashlock when he was fifteen and Donna was fourteen. They dated steadily until Donna cooled the romance and began dating other boys. Even though Donna had cut off the relationship, the two remained close and Felipe never let his feelings for her die. While at work one day, Donna doubled over in pain, and the doctors soon discovered that she was dying of degenerative heart disease. In actuality, Donna's heart was enlarged and growing. She desperately needed a heart transplant. Felipe heard about Donna's condition, and was devastated. In his heartache one night, he told his mother, Maria, "Mom, I love her. I'd do anything for her. Soon I'm going to die, and I'm going to give my heart to Donna." His mother said to herself, "Fifteen-year-olds say irrational things like this from time to time," and she thought nothing more of it. After all, Felipe appeared to be in perfect health. Moreover, she knew that Felipe loved Donna with all of his heart.

Three weeks later, Felipe woke up one morning and complained of a pain on the left side of his head. Suddenly, he began to lose his breath, and he couldn't walk. After arriving at the hospital, doctors discovered that a blood vessel in Felipe's brain had burst and left him brain dead. Felipe's situation mystified his doctors. While he remained on a respirator, his mother remembered what he had said—"I'm going to give my heart to Donna." His family decided to let the physicians remove his heart for Donna. His kidneys and eyes went to other people in need of those organs. Later that day, doctors successfully lifted Felipe's heart from his body and placed it into Donna's chest. After the operation, Donna's father told her that Felipe had evidently been sick for about three months before he died. He said, "He donated his kidneys and his eyes." There was a pause and Donna said, "And I have his heart." Her father said, "Yes. That was what he and his parents wished." Her expression changed and then she asked her father who knew. He told her, "Everybody." Felipe's father said, "It was something Felipe wanted to do for someone he cared for." Felipe understood "the Way." Felipe was willing to lay down his life for a friend. Now, Felipe lives on in the one he loved.

The story of Ahmed Ismail Khatib & family

I read a story online about some folks who understand living "the Way" Jesus intended even though they aren't Christians. The story was about a 13 year-old

Palestinian boy, named Ahmed Ismail Khatib. Ahmed was celebrating one of the holiest days in the Muslim calendar with his family in Jenin. Jenin is one of the most hotly contested areas in Palestine. Jenin City and its adjacent refugee camp are home to descendants of refugees expelled from Israel during the 1948 Arab-Israeli War. In a long history of tension, consistent violence has been the norm for years. Ahmed and his friends were playing with toy rifles when they were mistaken for militants. IDF troops proceeded to open fire on the boys and Ahmed was hit. The soldiers, realizing their mistake, rushed Ahmed to a nearby hospital in Haifa, Israel. Ahmed lay in the hospital for two days before finally succumbing to the fatal wounds.

As a father myself, I can't imagine what I would feel if someone shot one of my girls. I would be grief-stricken. I imagine I would move on to anger, if not rage. In addition, even though I don't know anyone that I have hate for, killing my daughter might just invoke that feeling within me. What a senseless tragedy. To die for playing with a toy gun is incredibly absurd. Knowing that your child is in the ground for such a pointless reason would be completely maddening for me. What's worse in Ahmed's case is that however inadvertent, it was the oppressors of his people who gunned him down. If I try to imagine my daughter dying at the hands of someone whom I am not overly fond of, I just become sick and furious. I wonder if God felt any of these feelings as those who had rejected him were murdering his Son.

Instead of reacting to his death with anger and grief, Ahmed's parents responded with extreme love. They decided to donate Ahmed's organs to needy Israeli children. This was radical for many reasons. First, Israel suffers from a shortage of organs. According to Science and Theology News, the consent rate for donation is about 45 percent. Jewish religious law prohibits the desecration of a dead body and requires that all body parts be buried. Organs for Israeli patients often come from Cypress, which has an exchange agreement with Israel—donated organs for trained surgeons. Israel does offer a financial incentive to families for donated organs. However, Ahmed's family only learned this incentive after they made the decision to donate his organs. Second, there are the religious differences between the two. Let's not forget, the enemy's children are the ones that Ahmed's parents decided to help.

Ahmed's heart saved a 12-year-old girl. His lungs sustained a 14year-old girl who suffered with cystic fibrosis. His kidneys went to a 5-year-old boy, a 4-year-old girl, and his liver to a 7-month-old girl and a 58-year old woman. All together, Ahmed saved six lives with his death. "I feel that my son has entered the heart of every Israeli." Ahmed's father, Khatib, told an Associated Press reporter. "It was to give a symbol of peace so that people could live together," Khatib explained to a BBC reporter. "Everyone knows that the olive branch is a symbol of peace, so instead of an olive branch, I have sewn the seeds of my son's organs inside the children of Israelis. We're talking about young children. Their religion doesn't make a difference," he said. Can you imagine? The love that that father showed the killers of his son goes past my comprehension. After reading this story, I couldn't help but think that this Muslim family is more "Christian" than most of us are. Ahmed's family received nomination for the Nobel Peace Prize in 2005.

When Jesus walked this earth, he taught by the way he lived. Most people couldn't understand him. The church didn't agree with his ways. Scholars of the Law hated his takes on real life issues. The disciples were often frustrated by his lessons and by his way. On rare occasions, though, some people understood. They 'got it.' Mother Theresa 'got it.' Ahmed's dad 'gets it,' Christian or not. Unfortunately, two thousand years later, most of us still don't 'get it.' I know there are many times when I find myself still missing the point. I look back over my life and I hate how often I have completely ignored the most glaring opportunities to make an eternal difference. I deliberately chose my own comfort and happiness over the feelings and needs of others. I'd love to have those old days of discontent, immaturity and misdirection back. I blew it repeatedly. I still catch myself doing it. So, how do we make sure that we 'get it?' It's nearly impossible to always be Christ-like. Obviously, equality with God is unattainable for us. To quote a dear friend of mine, "We suck at being Holy." It's true. We can't do the "Christian thing" very well. However, we can make a conscious effort to live the way he intends for us on a more consistent basis. The best advice I can give you now is to remember how often Jesus stressed putting others first and to worry about ourselves last. Moreover, Jesus wasn't just lecturing or presenting noble ideas that he would never stoop to himself. He exemplified his words in the way he lived and the way he died. Jesus walked the walk and showed us the way but we're still missing it.

The more I think about it and the deeper I dig, I come to a question that I believe to be the heart of the matter. At the same time, it almost seems trite. I want to challenge you with this question; do you love Jesus? This isn't Sunday school or a church class; so don't give the knee jerk predictable answer. Are you really in love with Jesus? It's easy to say, "yes," rather quickly, isn't it? Most people with any church background would certainly say, "What kind of question is that? Of course I love Jesus!" Really? As a kid, I sang songs in church like, "Oh How I Love Jesus" and "My Jesus I Love Thee," without really thinking about it. Then again, in my young dating life, I told several girls I loved them without really thinking about it. I've said things like, "I love the Miami Dolphins," "I love Sky-line Chili," and "I love the Beatles" too. Realistically, however, I've never met any of the Beatles. I like a lot of their music, but I don't love them. I've been a Dol-phins fan for over thirty years. I've spent excessive amounts of time watching them, reading about them and spending time with them at the many games I've attended over the years. Yet, I can't say I love them either. Not really. Conversely, I do love my wife. I'm not always the best husband but I love her. I love her increasingly as time goes by. Over time, I've come to know and understand her more. I love Brooke, Katie and Adrienne more than I love myself and that's something I know is true. I love my parents very much. Jesus? Hmmm. I think that I had an infatuation with him when I first met him. I would say I loved him without really thinking about it. I'd say I loved him but I didn't really know him. Not really. Do I really love Jesus? I can honestly say, "yes" now. It has taken me a long time. I'm not the best follower. I don't represent him well at all times. How-ever, over time, I've come to know and understand him more. In fact, I love him more than I love myself and that's something else I know is true. I have seen it play out increasingly in recent years (even in recent months). I do love Jesus. Very much.

What about you? Do you love Jesus? It is nearly impossible to "get it" or to embrace "the Way" until you do. Loving Jesus is a decision. Either you do or you don't. It's an everyday decision. It's not so unlike loving your wife or husband or boyfriend or girlfriend. What steps did you take to begin loving your significant other? What was the formula you used to begin your relationship? My guess is you took one look at them, and said, "Wow! That's who I want!" Alternatively, maybe you took one look at who they were and said, "Wow That's who I want!" On the other hand, perhaps you were eventually around them long enough to become "wowed." So many of us have tried to turn loving Jesus into a multiple step formula. Do this, this, this and this and then you will love Jesus and he will love you. The only problem with this approach is that it isn't biblical and it isn't Jesus. Now before you throw this book into your fireplace, trashcan or your dog's mouth, allow me to clarify. Obviously there are certain things that any follower of Jesus would do. One look at the Gospels and you can find tons of things that

Jesus (and his Father) find pleasing. Forgiveness. Faith. Baptism. Prayer. Serving. Mercy. Love. Sacrifice. Giving. Confession. Repentance. Telling others (from evangelizing to witnessing to making disciples). Loving Jesus. Loving God. Loving your neighbor. These are a few of the no-brainers. To take issue with any of them is to take issue with Christ himself. Good luck with that. I've had church leaders corner me on this before saying, "What are the essentials? What are the non-negotiables?" To which, based on Jesus' life and theology, I'd have to say ... "All of the above." From a biblical perspective, how do you argue against repentance? From a biblical perspective, how do you argue against baptism? From a biblical perspective, how do you argue against mercy? Giving? Loving your neighbor? We aren't going to be successful in every area of our relationship with Christ, but thankfully, our salvation is not primarily about on what we do. Rather, the foundations of our hope are things like God's grace and Jesus blood. Our faith in God's Word and Jesus' promises are the essentials, not church attendance pins or man's approval or theological degrees. It doesn't take too much time spent with Jesus before we have to say "Wow! That's who I want!" It is within the confines of that "Wow", that we can truly become what he wants. Christians. Difference makers. Servants.

That was his way—service. We are missing it. In my twenty plus years of travel, I have heard so many sermons that left me knowing everything the speaker was against and little, if anything, that he was for. This is why most people see Christians in a negative light that varies from the mildly suspicious to the completely disgusted. The time for movements and petitions and protests are over. It's up to every one of us who profess Jesus as our Lord to initiate personal revolution. The world will not be convinced that Jesus is the best option until Christianity produces the very best individuals. If you want to change some opinions, then really love your neighbor as you love yourself. If you want to turn some heads, practice tenderhearted mercy and kindness to others. If you really want to make a difference, serve. If you want to feed Jesus, feed the hungry. If you want to give Jesus a drink, provide for the thirsty. Visit those in prison. Take in the homeless. Look after orphans and widows. Care for the sick. These are the essentials. These are the non-negotiables. Consider Jesus' words starting in Matthew 25:31; *"When he finally arrives, blazing in beauty and all his angels with him, the Son of Man will take his place on his glorious throne. Then all the nations will be arranged before him and he will sort the people out, much as a shepherd sorts out sheep and goats, putting sheep to his right and goats to his left. "Then the King will say to those on his right, 'Enter, you who are blessed by my Father! Take what's coming to you in this kingdom.*

It's been ready for you since the world's foundation. And here's why: I was hungry and you fed me, I was thirsty and you gave me a drink, I was homeless and you gave me a room, I was shivering and you gave me clothes, I was sick and you stopped to visit, I was in prison and you came to me.' "Then those 'sheep' are going to say, 'Master, what are you talking about? When did we ever see you hungry and feed you, thirsty and give you a drink? And when did we ever see you sick or in prison and come to you?' Then the King will say, 'I'm telling the solemn truth: Whenever you did one of these things to someone overlooked or ignored, that was me—you did it to me.' "Then he will turn to the 'goats,' the ones on his left, and say, 'Get out, worthless goats! You're good for nothing but the fires of hell. And why? Because—I was hungry and you gave me no meal, I was thirsty and you gave me no drink, I was homeless and you gave me no bed, I was shivering and you gave me no clothes, Sick and in prison, and you never visited.' "Then those 'goats' are going to say, 'Master, what are you talking about? When did we ever see you hungry or thirsty or homeless or shivering or sick or in prison and didn't help?' "He will answer them, 'I'm telling the solemn truth: Whenever you failed to do one of these things to someone who was being overlooked or ignored, that was me—you failed to do it to me.' "Then those 'goats' will be herded to their eternal doom, but the 'sheep' to their eternal reward."

Now, maybe it's just me, but this sounds a little like he is talking about salvation. The whole heaven and hell thing is a dead give away. Jesus is once again talking about the greatness of serving all of mankind. *"Whenever you did one of these things to someone overlooked or ignored, that was me—you did it to me."* The way to heaven is not through ceremonies or formulas or man-made traditions and legalistic banter. You may find this hard to believe, but deep down, many people think that those are the paths to righteousness. They don't realize it but by way of their religiousness, they're no different from the goats that Jesus refers to in this passage. Moreover, certainly, they will be just as surprised. Many people attend church for years and never serve a single soul. They know the Word inside out yet they are unmindful to the intent of its content. Jesus said, *"I am the Way."* He also said that, *"no one comes to the Father except through me."* It's not about our religion or knowledge. It's not about works either. What? Isn't that contrary to the whole serving thing? That depends on your heart. I don't do nice things to prove that I love my wife or my kids. I don't have to. I do nice things for my family because of my love for them. Because I love them, I want to please them. I desire their happiness and welfare. Nothing you can do will make Jesus love you more than he already does. Remember, he died for you 2,000 years before you whimpered your first sound. If you really love Jesus, if you genuinely love him, your service will be a natural act because of that love. You will love others because of your love for Jesus. That was just his way. When you are in love with Jesus, you'll probably 'get it' more times than not. The more time you spend together, the more like him you'll likely become. It's about humility. It's about love. It's about serving and that is his way.

8

"SO, WHAT ARE YOU GONNA' DO ABOUT IT?"

You are going to have an effect on everyone you know. Originally, I planned to call this book; "Jesus never had his name on an office door." The idea came from his impact on people outside of religious settings. Jesus influenced the masses in his own day in three short years. People like the woman at the well, the blind, the crippled, the disciples (none of which were ministers or hired clergy), prostitutes, the thief on the cross, tax collectors and tons of 'sinners' in general. Jesus seemed to have a special ability with those who deemed unholy or lacking spiritually. Jesus wasn't condescending, judgmental, hateful or rude. Jesus usually served the people he touched and then spoke the truth to them. Admonishment is always easier to take when it comes from someone you know loves you. Just like Jesus or your minister or anyone who is effective in sharing the message of Christ, we each can influence the people we meet. We all have a ministry. We all have a story (or testimony). We all have scores of opportunities to encourage and inspire those around us every day. Our failure to do so can have devastating results for those whose salvation depends on our mercy, love and depiction of who Jesus really is and what he can do in our lives. I know this all too well. I want to share with you a true story that took place in my life that you may find hard to believe. I have changed the names of those involved in case any of their friends or family ever read this. I actually hope that the real people read this someday. I am not proud of this story but it is true and it broke my heart and changed my attitude about how I deal with those who are different. The story begins in 1981 and ends in the year 2000. Make no mistake; you will have opportunities to help people positively or negatively for him. What will you do?

1981

I was a seventh-grader at E. Russell Hicks Middle School. I wasn't much different from my classmates. I was trying to figure out my ever changing body and complexion, learning how to talk to girls and how to fight and I was constantly being cruel to everyone who wasn't considered cool. Being cruel is something that seventh graders are great at, and as much as I hate to admit this, when it came to immature cuts and juvenile cruelty, I was on the All-Star team. One of the worst things I was ever part of was something we all called "the money pit." This was one of the most brutal acts I've ever heard of, anywhere. Suffice to say, I don't look forward to talking to God about this one.

In our lunchroom, there were rows of tables where we would all eat each day. All of us except; the kids who didn't have lunch or couldn't afford lunch that is. Those kids always sat in "the money pit." It was a smaller triangular area encased by four or five steps that dug into the ground in front of a stage. It was almost like an orchestra pit. Nearly every day, the same cast assembled down there. The Dempsey twins, Carlos Brisbane, Jimmy Baxter, Martha Metz, Brian White and, of course, Daphne Simpson. Daphne was poor, dirty, socially inept and poorly dressed as were the others in "the money pit." My friends and I would always take our change and toss it into "the money pit" just to watch these poor kids fight for the money. One of us would flip a dime, then a nickel, another dime or a handful of pennies. Toss a quarter and it was on! Kids would literally dive on the quarters. They would come to blows. I kid you not. We laughed and laughed and laughed. I told you it was brutal. It was downright despicable. I hate that I did that, but I did.

Daphne got much more from most of my classmates and I. Her thick frame glasses, broken speech and strange scent were all the ammunition we needed. We made fun of her to her face, behind her back and to anyone who dared to be nice to her. That girl was sucker punched, hit in the back of the head with rocks, had her glasses broken, was provoked into fights (which were never fair) and decorated with "Kick Me" signs on a daily basis. I never physically harmed her but I think my words were probably more hurtful than the fists, feet and rocks that regularly struck her. I called her every sophomoric name in the book. I used vulgarities. I was the polar opposite of Jesus. I wasn't a Christian. I'd gone to church, heard about Jesus and had been baptized at a young age. I knew better, I just didn't know Jesus. Daphne certainly did not see a glimpse of him in me. I would not fully understand the ramifications of my detestable behavior and failure to be like Jesus to Daphne until years later.

2000

When my parents announced that they were taking in a foster child, I wasn't overly surprised. Growing up I always had foster brothers and sisters. Mom and Dad would take in kids every several months until their parents could provide care for them again or until their adoption. I was in student ministry in Florida when they called me. "How would you like to have a sister?" Mom asked. We usually had boys when I was a kid. I always wanted a sister. "You're not pregnant are you Mom?" I said to my fifty-something mother. She told me that they wanted my approval before bringing Molly home. I assured them that I thought it would be awesome. They proceeded and I was excited to come home for Christmas with some gifts for my new sister.

I came through the front door greeted first by my new, twelve year-old sister. She gave me a strong hug around the waist and displayed all the giddy excitement of an agitated Jack Russell. We had a great day, exchanged gifts and had dinner. That night Molly said, "I hear you went to South High." "Yeah, I did," I told Molly. She said, "When did you go there?" I said, "I was there from 83 till 86 when I graduated." Molly's demeanor became eager. She said, "I'll bet you knew my mom then." I was instantly intrigued. "Your mom went to South High?" "Yep," she said, "until 84." "What was her name?" I asked.

Have you ever ordered a sweet tea only to receive a Diet Coke instead? It's especially nice when you hate diet sodas. Do you know how it feels when you take that first sip? You're expecting this deadly sweet sugary refreshment and instead you get this nasty combination of carbonated liquorish and goat urine. That's what's really in a Diet Coke. Molly's next few words were a lot like that. "Daphne Simpson. Did you know her? What was she like? Were you guys friends?" Molly's words were like daggers. Each one stabbed my memory banks and brought back all of the horrible things I said and did to Daphne. What could I say? Saying, "I treated your mom like dirt. I showered her with insults and hatred because she was poor and dirty" didn't seem like the right thing to do. All I could muster was, "Oh yeah, I knew her, just not very well. She was always nice to me." That was all the truth that I could release. Molly said, "I don't know her that well either. She has a lot of problems. Nobody can ever seem to help her. I wish someone could. She's my mom and I love her anyway."

I went into my parents' bathroom with a mix of heartache, shame and nausea. To know that I was part of a ruined life and that I never helped was bad enough. Now I was calling Daphne's offspring my sister and attempting to show her love made me feel like a big, insincere phony. Molly knew I worked in the church and that I was a Christian too. I knew that she would have future visits with her mom back at the agency and wondered how that conversation would go. It would probably go something like this; Molly would say, "My new brother is a minister and a good Christian guy. You went to school with him Mom. Do you remember Tony Wolf?" Then Daphne would say, "Oh, you mean the same Tony Wolf that used to call me nasty names, throw change at me and laugh when people were kicking me? That Tony Wolf? He's a minister. So that's what Christians are like, huh?" My thoughts then went to Molly. She will definitely think that I am a hypocrite. She won't be so proud of me anymore. She may even hate my guts. In any event, it won't be good.

After that, I started thinking, "Who else have I treated terribly in my life? Who else have I destroyed with my comments? Is there anyone I should treat better now? Are there shut-ins I could visit? Can I give blood? Could I join the Peace Corps? Is it too late for me to become a monk?" It got ridiculous. I felt so awful. How could anyone treat someone else the way I treated Daphne and all of the others? I never realized how much of an effect I could have on others or how that would change them or those around them. Maybe being nice to Daphne wouldn't have improved her life situation but she certainly would've seen Christians differently ... and so would her daughter. I never found out what happened when they talked. Molly was only with Mom and Dad briefly before the agency moved her.

As I get older, I can't stress to you how important it is to make the most of every chance you get to touch others in a positive way. Paul gave this same advice to the church in Colosse' in Colossians 4 when he writes, *"Be wise in the way you act toward outsiders; make the most of every opportunity."* You never know whom you are going to meet or where they are in life. You never know when you are going to sit down next to someone who has a serious need. You never know when you are going to stand in line with someone who is wrestling with his or her faith. One thing is certain; every day we encounter his people and unlimited opportunities. What you do, what you say and how you treat people will make a difference. My wish for you is that it will be a positive one. My will is that you can plant seeds or water those that are already there. I hope that when you lay down in a bed for the last time you will have cared for many. I hope that when you're breathing your last breaths you can know that you did as much for others as you could have and I hope you feel content and that you can smile. I hope you can mull over your years and see how much you have changed and how often you served others. It'll happen fast. My wife and I recently sat and talked in our room one night and she said, "Isn't it crazy how fast Brooke (our three year old) has turned into a little girl?" I'm significantly older than my wife is. I said, "In a few hours she will drive out of this driveway and head to college." I thought about how quick I have gone from high school freshman to 'middle-aged man.' I told Laura, "This is going to sound a little gloomy, but that's life." I feel grateful because I've had an incredibly happy life. If I die tomorrow, I consider myself blessed beyond what most of you who read these words can imagine. Nevertheless, I can't say I did everything right. If I could go back, I would've treated most people differently. Better. I would have met more people. I would have stopped and tried to help more often. It goes by fast to be sure. I hope that you'll make the most of every opportunity.

I once read an old Mystic Proverb about making a positive difference. The mystic said, "I was a revolutionary when I was young and all my prayer to God was: 'Lord, give me the energy to change the world.' As I approached middle age and realized that my life was half gone without my changing a single soul, I changed my prayer to: 'Lord, give me the grace to change all those who come into contact with me, just my family and friends, and I shall be satisfied.' Now that I am an old man and my days are numbered, I have begun to see how foolish I have been. My one prayer now is: 'Lord, give me the grace to change myself.' If I had prayed for this right from the start, I would not have wasted my life." The mystic 'gets it.' Revolution starts within us, as individuals as we seek and understand God's will for our lives. Most of the time, that will require us to tune up what is under our own hoods.

Recently I spoke at a church that one of my college classmates in leading in Winston-Salem, North Carolina. Gene Woolard was always one of my favorite people my last couple of years at college. He was one of the only students who faithfully attended every one of our basketball games. At our home games, we'd always have a scattering of the other teams fans, a few of our professors, Pop's wife and our girlfriends as a fan base. Remember, Roanoke is a tiny school so our home games often felt like road games. Nonetheless, almost without fail, Gene Woolard would be in the stands. I'd come back to the dorm after the game and talking to Gene was always like having my own ESPN analyst to break down our performance (or lack thereof). Gene was a straight shooter and offered constructive criticism, which was much different from the light-hearted denigration we always received from our student body following any loss. When we'd lose, people would yell stuff at me as I walked back into Harold C. Turner dormitory. "You suck!" "You played like a woman tonight Wolf!" "Hey Tony, you guys stink!" There were so many uplifting people on our nice little Christian campus. Gene, however, always liked the way I played. He would point to certain things like missed free throws and turnovers, or the occasional air ball and remind me, but he also always told me that he liked my effort—even when we lost miserably.

Gene told me a story during my recent visit that I never heard before. We were talking after services and he told me that his church was struggling. He also told me that he had received offers to go to other churches in recent years but that he felt he was supposed to stay and serve the small gathering of believers God gave him. "For whatever reason, God wants me to serve these folks. We are really struggling. I have had some wonderful offers. Offers that would be more beneficial to my wife and daughter. But God keeps telling me to serve here." I was truly inspired. I knew that Gene's heart for service was bigger than mine was. I never feel badly when I meet someone like that; I get goose bumps. I stir inside. "It sounds like you have this figured out to me Gene," I said. "It isn't about bigger churches or better opportunities, it's about the ones that God puts in front of you today. Right where you are," I said. Then Gene told me something I never knew.

"I was in the military before I came to Bible College. They don't call it 'the Service' for nothing. I really learned what sacrifice and putting others first was all about in the Army. It was more humbling than you can imagine at times. So, when I came out of the service and headed for the ministry, service was all I knew. It was what I respected. I was all set to go to another school in Tennessee, but I had told someone from my church I would at least go check out Roanoke," Gene said. I was curious to hear where this story was leading. He continued, "My father and I made the trip out to eastern North Carolina and pulled up on the street in front of RBC. When we got out, we saw a man painting an older building behind the chapel. We walked over to ask him where to go and before long, we were all standing there, painting, laughing, sweating and talking together. An hour or so later, he directed us inside to admissions. As he opened the door for us, I said, 'It was great talking with you, what was your name?' He said, 'Oh I'm Bill Griffin, I'm the President here.'"

I was stunned. I knew President Griffin from my five years on campus. Gene said, "When I saw the President outside painting an old building in the summer heat, I knew that this was the place for me." How many of us would really do that kind of thing? Think about it. You are the President of the college. Wouldn't you just hire someone to do that? Higher positions don't involve grunt work, do they? I will tell you that for most men, there's no reason for such mindless toil. There's no reason unless you're in the business of molding young men. There's no reason unless you're modeling servant hood. There's no reason unless you are like Jesus. There's no reason unless you are here to "serve, not to be served." Hearing that story reminded me of my Junior year when I saw Bill Griffin's predecessor, former President George Bondurant cleaning windows on the third floor of our unfinished dorm. Drywall dust, dirt and sweat covered his old bib overalls and painters hat. President Bondurant was retired. He founded Roanoke Bible College in 1948, and with all due respect, he had to have been at least 125 years old. Nevertheless, there he was; A retired, elderly college founder and former President. A man who had started several colleges and many churches doing what he apparently had done his whole life. Cleaning windows? No. He was serving.

Bill Griffin changed Gene Woolard's life. He didn't do it with a well-researched sermon or philosophical advice. He didn't give Gene a big, fat check or direct him to a financial planner. He didn't sing him a song. Bill Griffin changed Gene's life with a paint brush, some perspiration and a servant's heart.

We are sidetracked so easily. We often miss the moment and we rarely seize the day. We usually don't take the "less of me and more of you" approach. We fail to see what he really wants. We tend to overlook obvious chances to make an impression for Jesus and, instead, focus on our own agenda or our own problems. I was in Kansas City once speaking to a large group of young people when someone said something I couldn't believe. My contact was an older woman who was wonderful with kids. One look at her ministry and you could see her passion and leadership ability. Her talent and ability with children were unquestioned. However, even the most gifted person can lose track of their goals and purpose occasionally. I had asked about the invitation time and how they wanted me to handle it. Her husband said to her, "Honey, if they want to make a decision, why not tell them to come talk to us after the program?" The lady looked flabber-gasted. She looked back at her husband and said, "Sweetheart, there are over 2,000 people here. Do you know how much I have to do tonight? I don't have time to talk to people about Jesus!" I almost cackled. I was sure she was kidding. I was sure until he said, "No, you're right dear. Sorry." She shook her head and looked at me as if to say, "Do you believe this idiot?"

In my many years of youth ministry and travels, that kind of thing happens more often than you would think. I once heard an elder say, "I don't know how Jesus did things but this is the way we do them!" Another time I heard a frustrated youth leader scream at some kids, "Shut the h___ up, we are trying to pray!" When I was between ministries and seeking an opportunity, a minister once told me, "When you're looking for a ministry, you've got to look out for yourself first." I could tell you a hundred stories just like these. We're too quickly dis-tracted from what God really wants from us. The enemy has ruined many a good man by messing with his focus. I see that everywhere I go too. I want to encour-age you to make your relationship with God number one. Make your life with Jesus your top priority; make your mark by serving others. Remember why you are here. God gave you an indescribable gift when he created you. Jesus valued you so much that he sacrificed himself for you. He has a purpose for your life and he wants you to use the ability he has given you. He wants you to serve. He wants to impact others through your obedience. He knows that lives will change if he can use you. He knows that with his help, you are capable of all things possible and impossible and you don't have to have a Masters degree in Theology to do it. Jesus never had his name on an office door. His impact occurred through his ser-vice. That is where your gifts will work in ways beyond all of your imaginings. In service, you will become an instrument of the one who is Lord and King and God over everything.

He hand painted you, sculpted you and supplied you with a case of talents that only he knows the depths and extents of. When I was in high school, I received an invitation to attend a vocational school for artists for the duration of my jun-ior and senior years. That's right. No English classes, no Biology, no History classes—only art. It was awesome. While I was there, I studied from a book called "Drawing on the Right Side of the Brain" by Dr. Betty Edwards. Without get-ting into the physical and mental aspects and theories of the book, the exercises we performed from it provided amazing results. Some students were in the class for their gifts in photography, others to be architects and others to be fashion designers. My skills were in cartooning and portrait artwork. Every student improved in unbelievable fashion over the few weeks as we went through the book and it's exercises. By the end of the course, classmates who admitted, "I can't draw stick figures," were drawing about as well as I could when we started the book. It just proves one thing; we are all capable of a lot more than we think we are. Michelangelo once prayed, "Lord, let me always desire more then I think I can do." He also once claimed that masterpieces are all around us; we only have to chisel away at the rough edges to discover them.

I see masterpieces all the time. I'm not referring to art; I'm talking about people. Everywhere I go I run into people who are simply amazing to me. I recorded a comedic music project a few years ago with an incredible producer and engineer. He has worked with or been connected to some of the biggest names in the industry, but you would never, ever know it. He's humble, welcoming and as genuine as they come, and his faith is evident in his life. He is the kind of man I hope my daughters will marry someday. With the highest respect to his craft, David Browning is a far greater person than he is a musician.

I met a seventeen-year old set of twins a year ago out in Arkansas. Michael and Mary Beth are the kind of people that you know God put on this earth specifically for his people. Michael sat with me one afternoon and told me that his father was discouraging his calling to ministry and pushing him towards the lucrative family business. We had a great talk and I told him, "Your dad just cares about you, that's all. Maybe he's right." He looked at me with shock. "Michael," I said, "I think it's obvious that God has big plans for your life. If you truly keep him first, he will use you if you are a student minister, a missionary, a business man, a doctor or whatever." Michael and Mary Beth are amazing young people.

One of my closest friends from high school and Bible College, Larry Simons, worked closely with me to improve the comic element in the dramas I wrote in college. His comedic input helped make those skits great. Larry has spent the majority of his post college life caring for the severely handicapped and troubled teens as well. To me, that is an awesome ministry. I know another girl, Jenni, who has helped start an organization called Sportable where individuals with physical disabilities can experience social interaction, physical fitness and athletic competition. She is reaching out to serve people with her passions and talents. I have numerous friends in the mission field in Africa, Japan, Indonesia and Russia to name a few. A dear friend who passed away a few years ago, Tom, was one of the most generous men I've ever met. Tom was a knee specialist and he was an elder in his church. One of the greatest Christians I've ever known, Ralph, worked for Siemens for most of his adult life while leading everyone around him by his example. Ralph showed me Jesus every time I saw him by the way he lived. One of my neighbor friends, Jeff, has a lucrative crane and hoist business that allows him to fund mission trips and other substantial needs of his congregation. Jeff also plays drums in the praise band at his church. My old friend Mark Lukhard, now a real-estate agent, is still introducing people to Jesus. Another friend, Kenny, is a bailiff and continues to minister to everyone he meets. My college friend Rick was a security agent and a church consultant before recently accepting a student ministry in North Carolina. My friend Peter, who helped out the boy in the highway accident, is running a company that installs sound systems and lighting in schools and churches. My old youth minister, Jay, is teaching character education in public schools. The Gettig's are nursing, teaching and fighting fires. My former minister Scott is still ministering at that church in Florida, and somewhere in eastern North Carolina, old man Alligood is still out there on a lawnmower … and I'll bet he is still molding people's lives too. All of these people have one thing in common; they love Jesus. They also are all using the gifts and passions God has given them in a positive way. Most of the time, as you can see, that translates into ministry on some level or another.

For now, I want to encourage you to be passionate about what you are doing everyday. Abraham Lincoln once said, "Whatever you are, be a good one." That means if you are a cook, prepare the best dishes that you can. If you're in construction, work each job as if you are building your own home. If you're a teacher, remember that you are instructing and molding God's children (especially the rough ones). Do each job like Jesus is your boss and God is the owner. In chapter 3, Paul tells the Colossians (verses 23–24), *"Whatever you do, work at it with all your heart, as working for the Lord, not for men, since you know that you will receive an inheritance from the Lord as a reward. It is the Lord Christ you are serving."* As your experiences grow, you'll be more prepared to serve God in the situations he places before you. God is working on you and through you every day. Some of you will serve him best right where you are, believe it or not. Others of you will eventually serve him in another capacity, vocation, city and state. A few of you will even serve him in another country. Strive to do the best you can, where you are, every single day. Don't look past the amazing opportunities that surround you right now, just look around. God will bless your efforts and he will decide when, where and what's next.

At the same time, be passionate where God has gifted you and be obedient to what he desires from you. He desires service and sacrifice and he wants you to use the remarkable talents you have. He wants your forte to be exposed and available to his people. He wouldn't have given you your gifts if he didn't want you to do something with them. That would be like giving your mom a football helmet to wear on her birthday. Unless your mom plays for the Rams, why would you do such a thing? Or saying to your four year old son, "Happy Birthday boy, here's your set of dentures." That would be a hit for sure. You wouldn't take a chainsaw to a baby shower would you? You wouldn't buy your Great Grandma a surfboard, would you? We usually try to give people things that are useful or that they enjoy. Your Father is no different. God has given us each abilities that are extremely useful to us. We should always strive to utilize them and sharpen them. If you have a talent for painting but you're a broker, don't leave your easel in the closet. Use the weekends or an hour or so at night to enjoy your gift and develop your skills; you never know when God may want to employ your expertise. The worst thing you can do is to bury the talents he has entrusted to you. Do you remember that parable? Here is another one for anyone who just decides to do nothing with the abilities God gives each of us:

The Parable of the Eagle and the Chicken

There once was an Eagle and a Chicken. The two were very close and spent much of their time flying together. One day, while high in the sky, the Chicken said to the Eagle, "Man, I'm starving! Let's go get some grub!" "Oh yeah, you can count me in," said the Eagle. So the two zeroed in on some animals eating in a pasture and decided to check it out. When they hit the ground and started eating, a nearby Cow said, "Hey guys, come get some of this corn, it's awesome!" The two birds were shocked that the Cow wanted to share. "You want to share with us?" asked the Eagle. "Why not?" said the Cow, "When it's all gone, Farmer Fran will just give us more." Given this information, they all feasted until the corn was gone. "Farmer Fran must be a nice guy," said the Chicken. "Oh, he is! And since he grows all of our food, we don't even have to work for it!" said the Cow.

"Alright, hold up," said the Chicken. "You mean to tell me that he just gives it to you?" "Yep," said the Cow, "and better than that, he even gives us a place to live too!" The Eagle and Chicken just looked at each other with their beaks agape in disbelief. They had always had to work hard for food and shelter. The Chicken looked at the Eagle and said, "Man, we get all the food we want without working and a nice barn that's warm and dry? I've worked my tail off for years; I'm staying. That's all there is to it, I'm staying."

"Listen Chicken," said the Eagle. "Doesn't this seem a little too good to be true? I mean, I've always been told nothing worth having is free. Plus, I like flying high and free. Finding food and shelter isn't so bad. I actually like the challenge." Nevertheless, the Chicken stayed even while his dear friend, the Eagle, soared away. Time went by and the Chicken was living large. He ate as much as he wanted, when he wanted as often as he wanted. He enjoyed free accommodations and he never worked.

One day he heard Farmer Fran tell his wife Frieda that he wanted some fried chicken for dinner. The Chicken finally put it all together and realized what was about to happen. He knew he had better fly away as the Eagle had months before. However, when he attempted to fly he found that he had grown too fat and lazy and in a matter of hours, he found himself headless on a plate next to some mashed potatoes and green beans. When you give up the challenges of life in pursuit of "security," you may give up your freedom. In addition, if you don't use your gifts, you may lose them.

Finally, there may even be gifts that you will have to discover by simply looking for them. I mentioned painting earlier. Anna Mary Moses, better known as "Grandma Moses," never started painting until she was 78! Yet, she managed to paint over 1600 pieces of art during her last 23 years of life. Her works would become critically commended and bring honors from Presidents. Connie Madigan, a defenseman for the 1972–73 St. Louis Blues, holds a record that will never be broken. At the age of 38, the rugged defender became the oldest "rookie" to make his NHL debut when he took the ice on February 1, 1973, vs. the Montreal Canadiens. Harland Sanders cooked chicken dinners for people at his service station in Corbin, Kentucky for years. It wasn't until the young age of 62 that he started his legendary restaurant, Kentucky Fried Chicken. It's never too late (or too early) to use your gifts in an amazing way. You are capable of the astounding when you use your God-given gifts, so be willing to try it. An old quote says, "Never be afraid to do something new. Remember, amateurs built the ark; professionals built the titanic." Never let anyone put limits on what you and God can do together. Leap from the boat. Focus. Walk on water.

Ultimately, how you use your gifts to serve others will be your legacy. It's your decision. You will decide each day how you will interact with others. Will you treat the less fortunate and the different with respect and thoughtfulness and kindness or will you act as though you don't have time for them? Will you use your time and abilities to serve a higher purpose or selfishly drop them into the ground hidden from sight or use? Will you diligently approach every opportunity as though you are working for a Holy boss or will you be fat and lazy, unable to fly, when it comes to soaring to the heights he created for you? Remember, in Ephesians 3:20 Paul writes, *"God can do anything, you know—far more than you could ever imagine or guess or request in your wildest dreams! He does it not by pushing us around but by working within us, his Spirit deeply and gently within us."* What can he do through you? How much can you imagine? Just how wild can you dream? Again, I implore you to think big and be a servant.

I didn't write this book in order to join the ranks of the self-helpers; there are more than enough of those to go around. My goal was to share my own experiences and the effect that they had on me. In truth, we need less self-help books and more selfless help books. The secret to create authentic happiness in your life is to serve, give and express love to others. In the words of the great theologian Paul McCartney, "And in the end, the love you take is equal to the love you make." What you get usually equals what you give. Since the extent of your service is completely up to you, you already have the key to your own happiness and fulfillment. What remains is for you to determine what you do with your key. Just remember who gave it to you.

As you have read this book, I'm sure you have discovered that I don't have all the answers. Anyone with an I.Q. over 62 must know by now that I'm no genius. I can't read the original Greek or Hebrew texts from which our Bible comes. However, I do know that my life's most important moments were the ones I spent helping others. From feeding my baby girls oatmeal to cutting up trees in Pass Christian to holding the hands of dying friends and acquaintances, I am finding my place in this world. I pray for that same clarity for you. I pray that God grants you wisdom and strength as you learn, by trial and error and in elation and grief, to serve. You and I have an awesome task and a beautiful chance to positively affect all those we meet. It isn't our responsibility to show them their mistakes or point out their sins. We are to show "the Way" by how we serve and how we love others. If we fail in this area, we might just as well keep our mouths shut about Jesus. We may as well forget teaching correct doctrine. We are wasting our time in church services on Sunday. No one will care. I want to close by offering you the same encouragement that Paul and Timothy gave the Philippians, *"Do not be anxious about anything, but in everything, by prayer and petition, with thanksgiving, present your requests to God. And the peace of God, which transcends all understanding, will guard your hearts and your minds in Christ Jesus."*

"A Prayer for Joy"

Help me, O God, to listen to what it is that makes my heart glad
And to follow where it leads
May joy, not guilt, your voice, not the voices of others, your will, not my willful-
ness,
Be the guides that lead me to my vocation.
Help me to unearth the passions of my heart that lay buried in my youth.
And help me to go over that ground again and again
Until I can hold in my hands, hold and treasure, your calling on my life.

Ken Gire, Windows of the soul

978-0-595-47341-0
0-595-47341-5

Printed in the United States
110585LV00002B/191/A